Warehouse Theatre Company's

Dick Barton
Episode III

THE TANGO OF TERROR

by **Phil Willmott**

Dick Barton, Episode III: *The Tango Of Terror* was commissioned by the Warehouse Theatre Company and the world premiere took place at the Warehouse Theatre, Croydon, on Friday 7 December 2001.

Warehouse Theatre Company Regd. Charity No: 272816

Supported by
CROYDON
COUNCIL

LONDON ARTS

D0432873

Dick Barton
Episode III

THE TANGO OF TERROR

by **Phil Willmott**

Dick Barton GEORGE ASPREY
BBC Announcer KIT BENJAMIN
Jock Anderson DARRELL BROCKIS
Daphne Fritters KATE PINELL
Juan El Bigglesworth DUNCAN WISBEY
Mrs Horrocks JOANNA BROOKES

All other parts are played by members of the company

Directed by TED CRAIG
Musical Direction STEFAN BEDNARCZYK
Musical Staging MITCH SEBASTIAN
Designer RUSSELL CRAIG
Lighting JAMES WHITESIDE
Stage Manager MARIE COSTA
Assistant Stage Manager JO HOTCHISS
Production Manager GRAHAM CONSTABLE

Casting SOOKI McSHANE
Press   (National) SALLY ANN LYCETT
            (Local) SARAH MALLETT

George Asprey Dick Barton

George trained at Lamda. His theatre credits include: Rolf in *The Sound Of Music*, Young Scrooge in *Scrooge* (World Premiere), Rusty Charlie in *Guy and Dolls* (National Tour), Darcy in *Pride and Prejudice*, Rudolpho in *View from the Bridge*, and Ellyot in *Private Lives*. His television credits include Sean Devreux in *Dying of the Right* (BAFTA Award Nominee), Jeremy Wells in *Coming Home* and its sequel *Naucherrow*, DC Hutchence in *Trial & Retribution*, Tony in *An Independent Man*, and *The Bill*. Film credits include *Mary Shelly's Frankenstein* and the soon to be released *A.K.A* and *Dead in the Water*.

Kit Benjamin BBC Announcer

Kit has just finished playing Colonel Gardner and the BBC Announcer in *Dick Barton* at The Nottingham Playhouse. Having been a music scholar at the famous Rugby School, Kit originally thought he was going to be a musician and, from his late teens onwards, was a conductor of a number of choirs and orchestras. At some point he changed his mind and, while he still maintains a number of musical interests, particularly in violin and singing, he has played a strange variety of characters on stage, both in musical and 'straight' theatre, from the psychopathic Sargeant in Kafka's *In The Prison Colony* to the androgynous role of Mary Sunshine in Century Theatre's national tour of *Chicago*. He toured for the same company in a rare revival of Noel Coward's *Bitter-Sweet*. Kit has also performed and recorded the title role in a new musical entitled *Isambard Kingdom Brunel*. Kit's most recent West End performances include *Cats* at The New London Theatre and *The Buddy Holly Story* at The Strand Theatre. He also spent a delightful two years playing Pat Levin, a role which he created, in Paul Elliott's production of *Jolson* at The Victoria Palace Theatre, on tour in the UK and at The Alexandra Theatre, Toronto.

Darrell Brockis Jock Anderson

Darrell Brockis trained at the Webber Douglas Academy of Dramatic Art after graduating from St. Andrews University. Darrell also appeared as Jock in *Dick Barton and The Curse of the Pharoah's Tomb* and the UK tour of *Dick Barton - Special Agent*. Previous stage roles include George Hughes in *Equiano* (Oval House and Tour); Herb in *Flow My Tears Said the Policeman*, Paul in *The Focus Group* (5th Column - Oval House); *Crash* (Warehouse); Jim O'Connor in *The Glass Menagerie* (BAC and Tour); Romeo in *Romeo and Juliet*, Lucenio in *The Taming of the Shrew* (RJ Williamson Prods., UK Tour); Hal in *Henry IV pts I + II* (5th Column, Edinburgh); Prince Ferdinand in the *Duchess of Malfi* (Byre). Darrell played Matthew Wargrave in Live TV's *Canary Wharf* and has made several short films.

Kate Pinell Daphne Fritters

Kate trained at the Liverpool Institute for Performing Arts, graduating in 1998 with a BA (Hons). She has performed as a soloist with the Royal Liverpool Philharmonic Orchestra and was very honoured to be asked to sing at Linda McCartney's Memorial Service at St. Martin-in-the-Fields. Kate has also sung at Buckingham Palace for the Queen, other members of the Royal Family and Tony and Cherie Blair. Kate played Lulu O'Donnell in the BBC Radio play *Not Aloud*. Her theatre credits include Fleur-de-Lys in *Notre Dame in Paris* (Dominion Theatre); 60's musical *Itchycoo Park* (National Tour) and *Puss in Blue Suede Boots* (Liverpool Everyman).

Duncan Wisbey Juan El Bigglesworth

Duncan is the sole surviving member of the original *Dick Barton* team and is a veteran of all three epsiodes, having played Lady Laxington, Sir Stanley Fritters and others in *Episode I*, and Swanker Of Arabia in *Episode II*. He first appeared at the Warehouse as Richard II in *The Court Jester*. This year Duncan has appeared in *Last Song of the Nightingale* (New End Theatre); *Over My Shoulder* (Jermyn Street Theatre) and *The Importance of Being Earnest* (Watermill Theatre, Newbury). Earlier appearances at the Watermill were as Petty in *The Government Inspector* and Simon in *Lloyd George Knew My Father*. He trained at The Central School of Speech and Drama. Other theatre includes *Forbidden Broadway* (West End); *Misalliance* (Vienna); *Under Their Hats* (King's Head, Vienna and West End); *Eurovision* (West End); *The Promise* (Orange Three, Richmond); *The Gingerbread Man* (Crucible, Sheffield); *This Happy Breed* (Farnham and Bromley); *Dick Barton Special Agent* (Warehouse Theatre,Croydon and on tour); *PVTV Wars* (Waterman Arts Theatre); *The Rise and Fall of Little Voice, Kiss Me Kate, Romeo & Juliet, The Go-Between* and *Charley's Aunt* (Norwich Playhouse's Premiere Season) and *The Frogs* (Nottingham Playhouse). Television: As a writer and also playing Paul McCartney and Alec Guinness on Alistair McGowan's *Big Impression* (winner Best Comedy Entertainment Programme at the British Comedy Awards 2000); *Peak Practice* (Carlton); *The Bill* (Pearson) and *The Hidden City* (Rough Film Productions). Duncan also takes part in rehearsed readings at the Globe and has worked as a musical director, composer and more recently as a stand-up comedian (which he doesn't like very much).

Joanna Brookes Mrs Horrocks

Joanna was born in London and trained at Webber-Douglas. Theatre includes productions at: The Redgrave Theatre, Farnham, York Theatre Royal, Leicester Phoenix, Southwold, Wilde Theatre, Bracknell, The Castle, Wellingborough, The Shaw Theatre, The Orange Tree, Richmond and most recently The Mill at Sonning Theatre where she played Sylvia in Jimmy Chinn's play *Sylvia's Wedding*. She has played many and varied roles including Sylvia in *Stepping Out*, Ruth in *Table Manners*, Hortense in *The Boyfriend*, and Hortensio in the UK and Australian tours of *The Taming of the Shrew* with The Medieval Players. Productions at the Warehouse: *Roister Doister, Hold On Hortense!, The Bells of Notre Dame, The Servant of Two Masters, Coming Up*, and the much acclaimed *Fat Souls* by James Martin Charlton in which she played Fat Mags. She also recently appeared in *The Beat 100 Plays of the Century* at The Royal National Theatre. Television includes: *Bergerac, EastEnders, The Bill, La Traviata, 5 Alive, Jo Brand Through the Cakehole, The Rory Bremner Show, People Like Us, Alistair McGowan's Big Impression, Peak Practice, The Thing About Vince, Numbertime, Grange Hill, The Inspector Lynley Mysteries*, John Mortimer's *Titmuss Regained* and Julian Mitchell's Screen Two film *Survival of the Fittest*. Radio includes: *Weekending, A Square of One's Own, House of the Spirit Levels, Kate and Cindy, Rent*, Harry Hil's *Fruit Corner, My Life as a Car, Paradise Lost in Cyberspace, Devices and Desires, The Worriers*, and most recently *Double Income No Kids Yet*. Films include: *Little Dorrit, Under Suspicion, The Fool and Harry Potter and The Philosopher's Stone*.

Phil Willmott Writer

Phil Willmott is 35, a playwright, director and actor and trained at Rose Bruford College. His work has won a London Fringe Award, the Brook Atkinson Award in New York, a Guinness Award for Theatrical Ingenuity and been nominated for a Peter Brook Award. He is artistic director of the Steam Industry and their base the Finborough Theatre and is an associate director of Battersea Arts Centre. Phil has directed over thirty productions around the UK from Shakespeare to cutting-edge new writing including recent hit productions of *Rent, Ring Round the Moon, The Grapes of Wrath, Geramine Greer's Lysistrata, The King and I, Crime and Punishment, Angels in America, Seven Brides for Seven Brothers, The Sound of Music* and his own adaptation of *A Christmas Carol*. Other work includes a studio season for the Open Air Theatre, Regent's Park, development of three new musicals with the Royal National Theatre studio, five productions at the Drill Hall and staging the London International Film Awards at the Café Royale. He has had eight plays successfully produced including, at the Warehouse Theatre, *The Castle Spectre* and the *Dick Barton* comedies.

Ted Craig Director

Ted is the Artistic Director and Chief Executive of the Warehouse Theatre Company. He commissioned the *Dick Barton* series and directed the original *Dick Barton, Episode I: Special Agent* at the Warehouse Theatre in December 1998. His production of this and *Episode II: The Curse of the Pharaoh's Tomb*, have been an almost continuous production since. Ted's career has included directorships of the Lyceum Theatre, Crewe, the Connaught Theatre, Worthing, the Drama Theatre of the Sydney Opera House and many freelance productions both here and abroad. These include the off-Broadway productions of *Look Back in Anger* with Malcolm McDowell (Roundabout Theatre); *The Astronomer's*

Garden by Kevin Hood (Warehouse and Royal Court Theatre); *Playing Sinatra* by Bernard Kops (Warehouse and Greenwich Theatre); *Sugar Hill Blues* by Kevin Hood (Warehouse and Hampstead Theatre); Shakespeare's *The Tempest*; Congreve's *Love for Love*; Moliere's *The Misanthrope*; Feydeau's *The Lady From Maxim's* (Sydney Opera House); *Tarantara! Tarantara!* by Ian Taylor (Theatre Royal, Sydney and Australian tour); *The Elephant Man* by Bernard Pomerance (Melbourne Theatre Company) and Arthur Miller's *The Last Yankee* and Joe Orton's *Entertaining Mr Sloane* (Theatro Ena, Cyprus). He co-founded the International Playwriting Festival and is proud of its considerable achievements in discovering and promoting new playwrights over the past 15 years.

Stefan Bednarczyk Musical Direction

Theatre credits, as an actor, include: *Semi-Monde* (Lyric Theatre, Shaftesbury Ave); *Dick Barton - Special Agent* (Croydon Warehouse and national tour); *Whenever* (Stephen Joseph Theatre); *Jermyn Street Revue* (Jermyn Street Theatre); *5 o'clock Angel* (Edinburgh, Hampstead, King's Head Theatres); *Laughter on the 23rd Floor* (Queen's Theatre, London and national tour); *Schippel the Plumber* (Greenwich); *The LA Plays* (Almeida); *The Game of Love and Chance* (Royal National Theatre); *Sugar Hill Blues* (Warehouse, Hampstead); *Playing Sinatra* (Warehouse, Greenwich); *A Midsummer Night's Dream* (Leicester); *A Midsummer Night's Dream* and *Twelfth Night* (Regent's Park); *Mozart and Salieri* (ATC); *Merrily We Roll Along* and *Noel and Gertie* (Cardiff); *Robert and Elizabeth* (Chicester). Musical direction has included shows at Chicester, Cardiff, Swansea, Leeds, Sheffield, Oxford, Regent's Park, Open Air, Buxton Opera House, Holders Opera Festival (Barbados), Warehouse Theatre, Croydon. Television credits include: *Crocodile Shoes, Crown Prosecutor, EastEnders, Love Hurts, Paul Merton - The Series, Harry Enfield and Chums, Stefan's Guide to Culture, The Grand Style of Jazz*. Solo cabaret performances include: *Seasons in London* (Pizza on the Park, King's Head Theatre, Jermyn Street Theatre) throughout the UK and abroad in Cannes, Antibes, Monaco, Cologne, New York, Los Angeles, San Francisco, Barbados and Vienna. Film credits include: *Topsy-Turvy, Composed, Sea Change and The Secret Diary of Bridget Jones*. Stefan has been the Musical Director of *Dick Barton - Special Agent* since the first production and is very grateful to the casts - past and present - for their contributions to the musical arrangements.

Mitch Sebastian Musical Staging

Mitch's work has received critical acclaim, particularly for the innovative way he has staged new productions of Broadway shows: *Pippin.co.uk.* (directorial debut) (Bridewell Theatre); *Romance Romance* (Gielgud Theatre); *Lucky Stiff* (Bridewell Theatre); *Merrily We Roll Along* (Royal Academy of Music). He is often associated with new works, collaborating with writers on original productions: *Watermark* (Crucible Theatre); *Eyam* (Bridewell Theatre); *Tales My Lover Told Me* (King's Head Theatre); *Hell Can Be Heaven* (Pleasance Theatre); *Twist Off Fate* and *Sing To The Dawn* (both for the Singapore Repetory Theatre). This creative drive has also led to Mitch being involved in many workshops in London and New York. He previously created staging for the Peter Hall Company's P*layhouse Creatures* (Old Vic Theatre); choreographed and staged the world premiere of *La Cava* (Victoria Palace, Picadilly Theatre) and the national tour of *Iolanthe* (D'Oyly Carte Opera Company). He was commissioned to stage a new oratorio *On The Eight Day*, by the London Philharmonic Orchestra and subsequently has staged several large-scale productions on their behalf. Mitch has directed and staged many gala concert performances all over the world, ranging from the hugely popular *Magic Of The Musicals* (London Palladium, European and national tours) to intimate cabarets such as *It Takes Two* (Jermyn Street Theatre) and *Three Lost Souls* (BAC and King's Head Theatre). He also staged Ria Jones' television special *For One Night Only* (BBC Wales) and Marti Webb's 1994 *Gershwin Concert Tour*. More recently he directed the Launch of Singapore's new television channel *TV Works*. After completeing a successful tour, Mitch's production of *The Rat Pack* celebrating the music of Sammy Davis JR, Dean Martin and Frank Sinatra is due to open in the West End.

Russell Craig Designer

Trained and worked in New Zealand. Opera companies he has designed for include ENO, Scottish Opera and Opera North. Operatic designs for ENO include *Seraglio Ariadne auf Naxos* with Giles Havergal, and *Count Ory* with Aiden Lang. Other notable productions include *Ariadne auf Naxos* for (ENO); *The Magic Flute* and *Boris Godunov* for Opera North; *La boheme* (GTO); *Hansel and Gretel* at the Grand Theatre, Geneva and *L'elisir d'amore* at La Monnaie, Brussels. Recently he designed *Tower*, the colliery opera, for Opera Box at the Swansea Grand. For musical theatre: *Bitter Sweet* for Sadlers Wells, London, *Show Boat* with the RSC and Opera North and the London Palladium, *My Fair Lady* in Minneapolis and Houston, and *Guys and Dolls* for Edinburgh Royal Lyceum. Notable drama work includes the *Taming of the Shrew* for the RSC, *The Rivals* for Manchester Royal Exchange and extensive work for the Unicorn Children's Theatre, where he is being made artistic associate. Russell is currently designing *Red Red Shoes* for the Unicorn and Place Theatre and *Oxygen* at Riverside Studios, London.

James Whiteside Lighting

James Whiteside graduated from The University of Birmingham in 1999. For the Royal National Theatre he has lit *Best Mates* (Site-Specific Tour) and *Urban Voices* (Albany Empire), and relit T*he Good Woman of Setzuan*

(Hall for Cornwall). Other theatre includes: *Rumpelstiltskin, The Gruffalo* (Tall Stories); *Nihil* (Warehouse, Croydon); *Bumps* (King's Head); *Othello* (Courtyard); *Twelfth Night, The Importance of Being Earnest* (Wimbledon Studio); *The Necklace* and *The Monkey's Paw* (Camden Peoples' Theatre). Opera: *Machinist Hopkins* (Queen Elizabeth Hall); *La Traviata* (Surrey Opera); *Matins for the Virgin of Guadalupe II* (BAC); *Sweeney Agonistes/Soap Opera* (Trinity College of Music). Musicals: *Little Shop of Horrors* (Derngate, Northampton); *Tommy* (HMP Maidstone). Future projects include *Orpheus in the Underworld* for Surrey Opera and a national tour of *Calamity Jane*.

Marie Costa Stage Manager

Marie trained at Mountview Theatre School before working as stage manager for the National Theatre of Cyprus. Since returning to England, Marie has worked as stage manager, company manager and production manager. She has worked as stage manager and sound designer on numerous productions at the Warehouse Theatre, including the International Playwriting Festival and Edinburgh Previews. She has worked with Sydney Theatre Company, Black Theatre Co-Op, The Octogan Theatre, Bolton, Paines Plough, Performance Theatre Company, Red Shift, Sphinx Theatre Company and Nuffield Theatre, Southampton. Other theatre work includes productions at the Drill Hall Arts Centre, Greenwich Theatre, The Young Vic Theatre, Riverside Studios, The Oval House, Brighton Festival and seasons at York Theatre Royal and The Thorndike Theatre, Leatherhead.

Graham Constable Production Manager

Graham studied stage design and performance at the Rijksakademie, Amsterdam, and under Josef Szajkna at the Studio Theatre, Warsaw. He returned to London and formed Arc, a mixed media performance group. Graham has constructed settings and properties for film, television and theatre, for companies as diverse as BBC TV, Venezuelan TV, the Edinburgh Wax Museum and Glydebourne Opera. As the Warehouse Theatre's Production Manager, he has built over 30 shows.

The Warehouse Theatre was founded in 1977 in one of Croydon's few remaining Victorian industrial buildings and soon built a national reputation for producing and presenting the best in new writing. In 1986 it launched the prestigious International Playwriting Festival. Having inaugurated a partnership with the leading Italian playwriting festival, the Premio Candoni Arta Terme, in 1995, selected plays from the International Playwriting Festival are now seen at the festival in Italy as well as at the Warehouse, offering the potential for further performance opportunities in Europe. Last year saw a new international partnership created, with Theatro Ena in Cyprus. Previous winners such as Kevin Hood, whose play *Beached* won the first ever Festival, have gone on to achieve incredible success nationally and internationally. Kevin's two subsequent plays for the Warehouse, *The Astronomer's Garden* and *Sugar Hill Blues*, both transferred, the first to the Royal Court and the second to Hampstead Theatre. His most recent work includes the BBC2 series *In A Land Of Plenty*. Andrew Shakeshaft's *Just Sitting* was selected in 2000, and was showcased in Italy and in London in 2001. A full production is being planned.

Today the Warehouse Theatre is acknowledged as one of the foremost theatre's for new playwriting in the country. Other hugely successful productions have included *Sweet Phoebe*, by Australian playwright Michael Gow, which saw the London stage debut of Cate Blanchett, *Iona Rain* (winner of the 1995 International Playwriting Festival) and *The Blue Garden*, both by acclaimed playwright Peter Moffat and last year's critically acclaimed *The Dove* by Bulgarian playwright Roumen Shomov. A continuing success is the company's stage version of *Dick Barton Special Agent* by Phil Willmott. First produced at the Warehouse in December 1998 it was an instant success, was brought back by popular demand in 1999 and has been on almost continuous national tour since. A new production opened at the Nottingham Playhouse September 2001. Dick Barton Episode 2 - *The Curse Of The Pharaoh's Tomb* was also an instant hit and a tour is planned.

WAREHOUSE THEATRE

Artistic Director Ted Craig
Administrative Director Evita Bier
Marketing Manager Sarah Mallett
Assistant Administrator Jenny Harrington
Education Co-ordinator Rose Marie Vernon
Box Office Manager Sharon Gomez
Production Manager Graham Constable
Stage Manager Marie Costa

Board of Management

Brenda Kirby *chair*, Cllr Eddy Arram, Celia Bannerman, John Clarke, Tim Godfrey, Dr Jean Gooding, Mike Hodges, Michael Rose, Mia Soteriou, Cllr Martin Tiedmann, Cllr Mary Walker

Patrons

Lord Attenborough CBE, George Baker, Lord Bowness CBE DL, John Gale OBE, Joan Ploright CBE, Robert Stilby JP

Funding Bodies

London Borough of Croydon
London Arts
London Borough Grants

Sponsorship

Warehouse Theatre Company are grateful for ongoing sponsorship from HSBC, Kingston Smith and Croydon Advertiser Group.

The Warehouse Theatre Company's International Playwrighting Festival
A National and International Stage for New Writing

This year the International Playwriting Festival celebrated sixteen years of discovering, nurturing and promoting the work of new playwrights, consolidating the role of the Warehouse Theatre Company as a powerhouse of new writing.

Plays are also presented in Italy at the leading Italian playwriting festival Premio Candoni Arta Terme. Many selected plays also go on to production in Britain and abroad. IPF 2001 marked a six year partnership with Premio Candoni Arta Terme and two year partnership with Theatro Ena Nicosia.

The Festival is held in two parts. The first part is a competition with plays entered from all over the world and judged by a panel of distiguished theatre practitioners. The second is a presentation of the best selected work from the competition, which takes place every November. Entries for IPF 2002 will be received from January 2002

Recent Successes

The Shagaround, the debut play by Southampton based playwright Maggie Nevill, was selected from the festival in 1999. The play was then showcased in Italian at the Premio Candoni-Arta Terme and at the Tricycle Theatre in English. The play, produced by the Warehouse Theatre Company and the Nuffield Theatre, Southampton has since toured at Nuffield Theatre (Southampton), Ashcroft Theatre (London), Soho Theatre (London) and Brighton Theatre Royal.

The Dove by Bulgarian playwright Roumen Shomov, selected in 1999, was produced at the Warehouse Theatre in April-May 2000, was showcased at the Premio Candon Arta Terme the same year, and went on to be produced twice in Bulgaria. "This fascinating play by Roumen Shomov...an accurate reflection of the lunacy of daily life" The Guardian.

Real Estate by Richard Vincent, selected in 1994, was produced in Italy by Il Centro per la Drammaturgia Contemporanea "H" in December 1999. It was also performed at 2 festivals in Italy last July - Quartieri dell'Arte and Festival delle Ville Tuscolane - and it will be produced at Teatro Colosseo in December this year. Richard has now received a commission from Granada Film.

51 Peg by Phillip Edwards, the 1998 Festival selection, was showcased at the Premio Candoni Arta Terme in Italy last May and received its British premiere at the Warehouse Theatre in October 1999, and was produced at the Edinburgh Fringe Festival 2000.

"Edwards' script is exceptional…goes beyond the norm that most playwrights would find comfortable" *Edinburgh Evening News*

"…an accurate reflection of the lunacy of daily life" *Evening Standard*

The Ressurectionists by Dominic McHale, the 1997 Festival selection, was premiered at the Warehouse Theatre in 1998, as a co-production between the Warehouse Theatre Company and the Octagon Theatre, Bolton. "Dominic McHale's entertaining debut…hilarious" Evening Standard

Just Sitting by Andrew Shakeshaft Premier at Premio Candoni Arta Terme 2001.

The selected plays for the International Playwriting Festival 2001 were *The Cobbler* by Bryan Delaney, *Six Black Candles* by Des Dillon, *Glory Days* by Amelia Morrey and *Knock Down Ginger* by Mark Norfolk.

The Shagaround   The Dove   Sweet Phoebe

First published in 2001 by Oberon Books Ltd.
(incorporating Absolute Classics)
521 Caledonian Road, London N7 9RH
Tel: 020 7607 3637 / Fax: 020 7607 3629
e-mail: oberon.books@btinternet.com

A catalogue record for this book is available from the British Library.

ISBN: 1 84002 265 5

Cover illustration: Peter Holt

Printed in Great Britain by Antony Rowe Ltd, Reading.

Characters

BBC ANNOUNCER

DICK BARTON

SNOWY

JOCK

COLONEL GARDENER

WILCO

RODGER

DAPHNE FRITTERS

JUAN EL BIGGLESWORTH
aka THE LATIN LOVE THUG

EFIL STRANGER

BBC FLOOR MANAGER

GENEVIEVE, BBC PRESENTER

MRS HORROCKS

CONCHITA HORROCKS

SIGNORITA YVETTE

SIGNORITA MAUREEN

SIGNORITA MARGARITA

SIGNORITA CASSANDRA

AIRPORT TANNOY

Musical Numbers

Act One

WE GLORIOUS FEW
　　Music: 'Jerusalem'
　　Dick, Colonel Gardener, Jock

NEVER TRUST A MAN
　　Music: 'Sunny Spanish Shore', *The Gondoliers* by Sullivan
　　Daphne, Jock

SNOWY AT THE OPERA
　　Music: 'Queen of the Night', *The Magic Flute* by Mozart
　　Snowy, Dick

THE LATIN LOVE TRAIN
　　Music: 'L'amour', *Carmen* by Bizet
　　Juan, Mrs Horrocks

SPECIAL AGENT COOL
　　Music: 'Early One Morning', Traditional
　　Dick, Snowy

SETTLING SCORES
　　Music: 'After the Ball is Over' by Charles K Harris
　　Juan, Stranger

Act Two

I LIKE-A-YOU
Music: 'Under the Bamboo Tree' by Bob Cole
Genevieve, Dick

THE CALL
Music: 'The Sleeping Beauty' by Tchaikovsky
Mrs Horrocks, Jock, Dick

EINE KLEINE TANGO
Music: by Mozart, arranged by Stefan Bednarczyk
Maureen, Margarita, Yvette, Cassandra, Jock, Conchita

NOTES TO SING
Music: Traditional
Rodger, Wilco, Jock, Margarita, Cassandra

ACT ONE

BBC ANNOUNCER: This is the BBC broadcasting from London, it's six forty-five and time for the next exciting instalment of Dick Barton, Special Agent! (*We hear the Dick Barton theme: 'The Devil's Gallop'.*) In our last episode, sharp sleuthing listeners will recall how our hero, Dick Barton, on a routine mission, ably assisted by his jolly working class sidekicks Jock and Snowy, had penetrated a long forgotten tomb deep beneath the surface of an Egyptian mountain side, to safeguard a legendary ruby from the forces of EFIL as led by a schizophrenic German *femme fatale* possessed by the malignant spirit of a long dead Egyptian showgirl. So, just your average Wednesday then – until an employee of London's very own British Museum, corrupted by unwholesome passions for the foreign strumpet, led an army of heavily armed homicidal lepers to surround the tomb, surely signalling certain death for our lads.

Scene 1

Egypt.

DICK BARTON: Not to worry, chaps. We'll make our way to safety through the underground catacombs.

BBC ANNOUNCER: But fate struck a further cruel blow, as the subterranean passages filled with foul smelling crocodile infested waters.

DICK BARTON: It looks like our only hope is to climb upwards through the maze of secret tunnels, navigating our way towards daylight by minutely analysing the direction of the air currents.

BBC ANNOUNCER: Imagine our heroes' disappointment, as they hear the native heathens prepare to pour boiling lava down upon then through those same passages.

DICK BARTON: Keep moving forward, lads, it's our only hope.

JOCK: DB, the way forward is blocked by a wall of deadly vipers.

DICK BARTON: Back men! Back! We'll have to fight our way out of this one with honest British fisticuffs.

JOCK: It looks like they've got reinforcement's back there. Boss, the foreigners are stacked up twenty men deep. There's no escape. We're dead men.

BBC ANNOUNCER: (*Packing up to go home..*) Well, that's that then. Thanks for listening over the years. We've had a lot of fun, haven't we? I suppose it's the shipping forecast for me now, maybe the occasional book at bed time. I was once head-hunted for Muffin the Mule, you know.

DICK BARTON: Hold on a mo!

BBC ANNOUNCER: But wait!

DICK BARTON: The foreigners are looking pretty mean, you say?

JOCK: Och aye boss, there's a look of pure evil about them.

DICK BARTON: I've just the ticket!

(*Quick burst of 'Rule Britannia'.*)

Scene 2

Lords cricket ground.

BARTON, JOCK and COLONEL GARDENER watching a match.

JOCK: Och! It's good to be back in dear old Blighty, DB.

DICK BARTON: Yes, and where better to spend a summer afternoon, than this bastion of British fair play – Lords Cricket Ground.

JOCK: I'll get the ices.

DICK BARTON: Good show.

(*JOCK leaves.*)

COLONEL GARDENER: Dashed clever of you to realise those Egyptian terrorists would let you go in exchange for tickets to the final day's play.

DICK BARTON: Not really, Colonel. Everyone knows there's only one thing foreigners like better then seeing

an Englishman in peril and that's seeing him getting
thrashed at cricket.

COLONEL GARDENER: Well, the blighters won't be
disappointed today! Our lads are making a pretty poor
show of it out there. (*Calls politely to the cricketers.*) Come
on chaps, get a wiggle on!
(*SNOWY arrives.*)

SNOWY: (*Yells at the cricketers.*) Ere! You lazy good for
nothing bunch, get your bleeding fingers out and wallop
a few into the stingers.

DICK BARTON: Snowy, go and help Jock with the
threepenny cornets, will you?
(*SNOWY leaves.*)

COLONEL GARDENER: The lad's got rather above
himself since they took the bandages off his face.

DICK BARTON: You could be right, Colonel. There's no
denying that disfiguring facial rash he developed two
episodes ago, following Baron Scarheart's fiendish
attempt to pollute Britain's tea supply, has actually made
him better looking.

COLONEL GARDENER: Even odder, he's now a foot
shorter.

DICK BARTON: Best not to dwell on the mysteries of
modern medicine, Colonel.

COLONEL GARDENER: Especially since anyone tuning
in for the first time won't have a clue what we're talking
about.

DICK BARTON: Quite so.

COLONEL GARDENER: Well, I suppose you'll be
looking forward to a well earned rest now that another
member of EFIL is safely behind bars.

DICK BARTON: Marta Heartburn got her just deserts, and
Piggy Petherington too, but the Society of Evil
Foreigners In London won't rest for too long, I'll be
bound.

COLONEL GARDENER: Quite right. We must stay
vigilant against EFIL. What makes them do it, do you
suppose? Is it simply jealousy that makes them grope for
our assets?

DICK BARTON: Who can say, Colonel, who can say?

COLONEL GARDENER: You'd think they'd know by now that we Brits are invincible.

(*A groan from the crowd as another England cricketer is bowled out.*

SNOWY and JOCK return with ice cream.)

SNOWY: Cor blimey! He's not out already is he? (*Yells to them.*) I've seen kiddies bat better on the beach at Margate. (*To BARTON.*) Here's the ice cream, Guv. D'you want me to fetch the car?

DICK BARTON: Perhaps you'd better, Snowy, old chap. It breaks an Englishman's heart to watch our men go down like this.

SNOWY: It does that and no mistake.

(*He leaves. A roar from the Egyptians.*)

COLONEL GARDENER: Listen to those foreigners jumping for joy at our chap's misfortune. Honestly, we bring 'em over here, give 'em every opportunity. The least they can do in return is support our cricket team.

DICK BARTON: Let's give the next man in a rousing cheer. Hoorah!

(*The sound of ball on bat. 'Howzat'. They flinch. Then sing.*)

We Glorious Few

From coast to coast we glorious few
Stood tall and proud
An empire grew,
In every land
A force for good
Where ere fair play was understood
We served the crown on bended knee
We made the world
Our Colony
With justice swift in its dispatch –
Why can't we win a cricket match?

We gave the world democracy
Alvar Lidell
The BBC

Wellington boots
And Vera Lyn,
Tuberculosis, Spam and gin
Shakespeare was British wasn't he?
Like Yorkshire pud and milky tea
With so much talent at our call
Why can't we hit the bloody ball?
Why can't we hit the bloody ball?
(*Everyone leaves the stage except JOCK and DAPHNE. Very Brief Encounter.*)

DAPHNE: Jock?

JOCK: Daphne?

DAPHNE: Oh, Jock!

JOCK: Oh, Daphne!

DAPHNE: I feared you wouldn't recognise me.

JOCK: Why of course I do, you bonny lass. It's Daphne Fritters. Only daughter of our Minister for Rationing, Sir Stanley Fritters.

DAPHNE: Oh Jock, can you forgive me for breaking your heart so cruelly two episodes ago?

JOCK: Och, of course I can. A fortnight's a long time in light entertainment.

DAPHNE: And you and you chums were so brave rescuing Daddy and I from the clutches of EFIL. Thank heavens you've forgiven my cold-hearted ingratitude.

JOCK: Och, forget it. It's not as if I've stayed up night after night trying to cry myself to some kind of tortured sleep, after day after day of hoping you'd just return one of my phone calls.

DAPHNE: I'm so glad we can put it behind us.

JOCK: Agony after agony every time the doorbell rang, praying that maybe one day you'd respond to my letter, that one day your butler would let me wipe my rough working men's boots at the doorstep to your heart.

DAPHNE: It's best to move on, isn't it.

JOCK: Everywhere I looked I saw your bonny face in the crowd, heard your voice in the birdsong of the sweet dawn chorus heralding another comfortless day without you. Last Saturday I thought I recognised your shapely form in a pickled walnut.

DAPHNE: Oh Jock, I was so wrong to spurn your wholesome working class affections. A pickled walnut?

JOCK: Quite so, miss.

DAPHNE: Heavens! If only we'd been stepping out together. I wouldn't be in the terrible mess I'm in now. Oh Jock, you've got to help me. You're the only one I can turn to.

JOCK: Anything, you wee timorous lassie. I'd do anything for you. Now what's the trouble? Do you need someone to rub linseed oil your lacrosse racket again?

DAPHNE: Oh Jock, it's far more serious then that. I'm afraid... I'm afraid I've made a bit of a fool of myself. I put my trust in a foreigner!

JOCK: Those devils, the boss said it wouldn't be long before they were up to their old tricks again. What happened, missy?

DAPHNE: I've been such a fool. I've fallen for the oldest trick in the book.

JOCK: Not the one where they put the girl in a box and pretend to saw her in half?

DAPHNE: Not that sort of trick. I speak of *l'amour*.

NEVER TRUST A MAN
(*Sings.*) When a whiff of his pomade
Filled the Burlington Arcade
I turned and caught his eye
And the sparks began to fly
Held there captive in his glance
I was lost, without a chance
When he asked me out to dance

But I'll never, never, never trust a man again
Never, never, never never – if I can again
Never, never, never, never
Never, never, never, never
Trust a man again.

As we danced the night away
In the Hammersmith Palais
I did not suspect a thing
As he stole my diamond ring
He was not all he appeared
When he nibbled on my ear
Both my earrings disappeared

And I'll never, never, never trust a man again
Never, never, never never – if I can again
Never, never, never, never
Never, never, never, never
Trust a man again.

When I saw his manly chest
I just had to look my best.
Yes, we women can be fools
I went out in mummy's jewels
Daddy's going to take this hard
And I can't tell Scotland Yard
Or my reputation's tarred.

And I'll never, never, never trust a man again
Never, never, never never – if I can again
Never, never, never, never
Never, never, never, never
Trust a man again.

Urgh! That brute! When I think of his cruel caddishness, that infernal tune he's always whistling, his broad manly shoulders, this handsome profile, his trim natty waist, his…

JOCK: You're right, missy, he sounds like a monster. Tricking you like that, when you were probably emotionally vulnerable from splitting up with me. Probably. Emotional vulnerable. What with us splitting up and everything.

DAPHNE: Oh Jock, what shall I do?

JOCK: Have no fear. You can rely on Dick Barton and the team to untangle this one.

DAPHNE: Oh Jock, no. I beg of you. I can't risk anyone finding out but you. Not even Mr Barton. Do you think it could be our little secret? I know you can track down this fiend and get my jewellery back.

JOCK: Well, I'll do my best, lassie. If only we had a clue to go on.

BBC ANNOUNCER: If only. The women of Britain are in desperate peril. Ladies, hang on to your handbags. When a foreigner's fixed his fiendish thoughts on foraging, there's no knowing where it'll lead. Meanwhile, top Secret Agents and show tune aficionados, Rodger and Wilco, are desperately trying to get in touch with Dick Barton.

(*We see RODGER on the phone. WILCO's voice is heard from off.*)

RODGER: I'm not getting any reply, Wiggy.

WILCO: (*Off.*) Well, keep at it, Rodg. We've got to get through to him.

RODGER: Darling, can't you take over for a while?

WILCO: (*Off.*) Not if you want me to have your shirt ironed for the Interpol dinner and dance, I can't. I've only got one pair of hands.

RODGER: Understood, Wigglet. (*Down the phone.*) Come along, Dicky, old boy.

(*A phone rings.*
SNOWY enters, trying to figure out where the ringing noise is coming from. Eventually he holds a cricket ball to his ear and speaks into a protective cricketer's box.)

SNOWY: 'Ello?

RODGER: Dick, is that you?

SNOWY: No, it's Snowy. The boss has just gone into bat. He's England's last chance of whacking back some foreign googlies.

RODGER: Fancy. (*Beat.*) It's Rodger here, of Rodger and Wilco.

SNOWY: All right, mate? I didn't think much of the new Lapino Lane musical at the Adelphi, did you?

RODGER: No time for chitter chatter now, old duck. Your
boss is in desperate peril. We have it on the best
authority that a brilliant criminal mastermind is heading
for Blighty, might already be in London. They call him
the Latin Love Thug. He's already decimated St Tropez,
Monaco, and anywhere where there's jewellery to be
swiped. It seems he can't help himself. Compulsive sort
of thing.

SNOWY: Sounds more Scotland Yard than us.

RODGER: Well, that's the thing you see. Our sources tell
us that he's just been recruited by EFIL, his mission is to
swipe a dossier containing the locations of British secret
agents all over the world. I don't mind telling you, Wilco
and I are very worried. Only last night a strange man
approached us with a pistol in his pocket.

SNOWY: Cocked?

RODGER: I should say so. If that file gets into the wrong
hands, EFIL could wipe out the entire British secret
service. One thing's for sure, he's going to want you,
Dick and Jock out the way.

SNOWY: I'll keep a look out. What's he look like?

RODGER: You'll find him anywhere there's beautiful
women with fabulous jewellery. He's a handsome devil,
apparently. Left a string of broken hearts all over the
continent. The only thing we know for sure is, he
whistles this tune.

SNOWY: It's no use telling me, I can't sing to no one. Hold
on a minute I'll get Jock.

RODGER: No time, I'm afraid. Wilco's giving me the
emergency signal. Either that or he forgot the oven
gloves taking the quiche out of the oven. Now just
concentrate. It's very simple.

(*He sings The Tune.**)

SNOWY: Yes, yes. I think I've got that. G'luck. Over –

RODGER: – and *out!*

(*JOCK joins SNOWY.*)

JOCK: How ye doing there, young Snowy?

* The Tune is that piece which non-pianists always bang out on the piano,
the notes of which can be found in the song in Act Two, Scene 8.

SNOWY: Shut up a minute, Haggis. I've got to concentrate. Think I've got it. Listen carefully, do you recognise this tune?

(*He sings a toneless din.*)

JOCK: Yes, of course I do.

SNOWY: You do. Crikey.

JOCK: It's exercise one from 'Bagpipes for Beginners'.

SNOWY: Do many swarthy Latin lothario types take up the bagpipes?

JOCK: It's more your fat, pasty, redheads on the whole.

SNOWY: I thought so. This is hopeless. I'm supposed to sing DB a very important tune that could mean life or death to British secret agents all over the world. I can sing if it's only me there, but any time I've ever tried to sing in front of everyone else, I get all panicky and I can't remember a note.

JOCK: I'd like to help you but I'm on a mission myself. It's an affair of *l'amour*. Can you tell DB I'll be gone a wee while and let Mrs Horrocks know I won't be in for supper?

SNOWY: Thanks for bleedin' nothing.

JOCK: Sorry Pal. (*Goes.*)

SNOWY: It's always been the same. Even in the school choir at Hornsey Road Infants, whenever anyone's watching I can't remember a note.

(*JUAN EL BIGGLESWORTH enters, whistling The Tune.*)

SNOWY: Juan? It's Juan El Bigglesworth, isn't it?

JUAN: (*Latino accent.*) I'm so sorry, I don't know what you're talking about.

SNOWY: Yes, you do, Juan El Bigglesworth. Your dad used to be the organist at the Gaumont Cinema, Elephant and Castle. 'Ere, that was a terrible business. I'm glad to see you picked yourself up.

JUAN: Thank you. It's…?

SNOWY: It's Snowy, Snowy White. We used to kick a can round the back of the gas works.

JUAN: (*Cockney.*) Snowy me old mucker, is it you? Cor blimey, it's been a while.

SNOWY: Look at you in your fancy clobber. You look like a right nob. You've obviously come up in the world. The last I heard you was doing time for knocking off a jewellers in Bermondsey. Obviously inherited your mum's eye for a bit of tomfoolery, eh? When'd they let you out?

JUAN: I did me time all right, but it was the best thing that ever happened. I learnt a lot of nifty moves, I can tell you.

SNOWY: I've heard people call prison the university of crime.

JUAN: Who gives a monkey's! I could never get interested in the best way to crowbar open a safe. I'm talking about ballroom dancing.

SNOWY: Eh?

JUAN: Yeah, I was the star of the E Wing ballroom and formation dance combo. You should see me on the floor! And with my looks, when I got out, I got plenty of work in the dance halls of Europe. Always plenty of little darlings looking to make two to tango, and they're pretty generous with their thanks, I can tell you. Picked up plenty of sparklers for me old mum then, all right.

SNOWY: Working abroad though, you must meet a lot of foreigners. Wouldn't suit me. Mind you, your ma had a bit of Spanish in her, didn't she?

JUAN: Course she did. That's where I got the looks. The birds go crazy for it. They reckon I'm Argentinian, Spanish, Brazilian… I just go along with whatever they fancy. Anyway, what are you doing with yourself these days?

SNOWY: Bit of this, bit of that, ducking and diving, wheeling and dealing.

JUAN: Course you do.

SNOWY: And then in me spare time, I work for MI5.

JUAN: Nice. 'Ere you might be able to help me. You don't know that Dick Barton, do you?

SNOWY: What, the special agent and tea time wireless celebrity?

JUAN: That's the one.

SNOWY: I should say so. That's him out there, batting.

JUAN: (*Looking.*) Blimey. He's good, isn't he. Well, he looks busy at the moment and I've got a hot date over Hatton Garden way. Shame. I've got a spot of business with Mr Barton.

SNOWY: Well as it's you, I'm sure he won't mind me giving you his HQ address. (*Gives him a card.*) I'll tell him you'll pay him a call.

JUAN: Yeah, why don't you do that. Thanks, matey. We'll have a proper catch up soon, eh? (*Leaving, whistling his tune.*)

SNOWY: Yeah, good to see ya, go careful.

(*The crowd applaud a Barton shot.*)

Well done Guv! Blimey, looks like it's going to be a long innings. Good job. He's going to be really cross with me if I can't sing him the code tune...

Snowy at the Opera

(*Sings.*) I'm in a spot. Can't sing with people list'ning.

Gawd, I'm a plonker.

I don't know how I'll teach DB that tune.

Course in the bath

My singing skill is really quite astounding

And I could be on stage performing Opera

It's just with people near I freeze with fear.

(*He puts thimbles on his fingers.*)

It's such a shame

Covent Garden's lost a star.

(*Pulls out a washboard and accompanies himself as he sings 'The Queen of the Night' chorus on 'lah' – but with the style of Chas and Dave. Finishing with...*)

They'd rewrite each show for me.

Suddenly the Barber of Seville could move to Bow

Suddenly we dump the magic flute and play the spoons

And a Carmen set in Catford would be sure to draw a

crowd

Or else a cockney Rigoletto'd do us proud

If only I could sing out loud.

(*Someone passes; he goes out of tune on the last note.*)
Oh well.
(*A gasp from the crowd. He calls to BARTON.*)
Nice Shot, Guv!
(*He exits sadly.*
DICK BARTON is standing at the crease.)
DICK BARTON: (*Sings.*) Last into bat and Britain holds it's
breath now

Starved long of Glory,
Our once proud nation hangs
It's head in shame, so here I wait,
The hopes of every Englishman are with me
So this is how it felt aboard the Vict'ry
It's Agincourt and Waterloo that's plain
Oh dear, that's rain
To the pavilion again!
BBC ANNOUNCER: (*Sings.*) Have the foreigner's
unleashed their voodoo tricks
So that rain stops Barton knocking them for six?
For meanwhile, whilst our hero tries to even up the score
At home a ruthless criminal is at his door.
Mrs Horrocks do stand sure!

Scene 3

DICK BARTON's HQ.

MRS HORROCKS is dusting, humming the theme from 'Housewife's Choice'. The doorbell rings. The usual two tones, but then it continues into The Tune.

MRS HORROCKS: Whatever's the matter with that
doorbell. It hasn't been the same since the Bulgarian
Ambassador got his finger stuck in it during the mystery
of the Bearded Lady of Dead Man's Crag.
(*JUAN bursts in to the room.*)
JUAN: (*Latino accent.*) Good afternoon, lovely lady.
MRS HORROCKS: No, the housekeeper – Mrs Horrocks.
You can't come in here, this is Mr Barton's private study.

This is where he keeps all his private things. Even I have to look away sometimes, I really do.

JUAN: Forgive this intrusion, but some exotic fragrance led me to your side.

MRS HORROCKS: That'll be the Brasso. I like to give everything a rub down every Tuesday and Thursday.

JUAN: No no, something else. There's something imperceptible, strong yet feminine about this room, comforting yet strangely exotic.

MRS HORROCKS: Don't ask me what they get up to in here of an evening.

JUAN: The fragrance – it's, it's you. Won't you share it's mystery with me?

MRS HORROCKS: Carbolic's in the soap dish love, help yourself. Now it was Mr Barton you wanted to see, was it?

JUAN: I once thought so but now I meet you, I'm not so sure.

MRS HORROCKS: I'm no special agent, but I've picked up enough tricks over me years as Mr Barton's housekeeper to spot that you're a foreigner. They're always trying to sneak in here to booby trap the pencil sharpener or leave sharp objects in the stationery draw. So either you're up to mischief, or…

JUAN: Or?

MRS HORROCKS: You're selling something.

JUAN: (*Looking out of the window.*) My goodness me. There's a naked man waving up at the window.

MRS HORROCKS: It's probably Mrs Crabshaw's eldest. I knew it was a mistake to reduce his medication. Where is he? He'd better not be at my herbaceous borders.
(*JUAN speaks into his wrist watch.*)

JUAN: Love Thug to HQ, Love thug to HQ. I'm in his headquarters with the bomb now. I've just got to distract some old biddy, then I'll plant it, scarper and it's, *Bye bye, Barton.*

MRS HORROCKS: Well, I can't see him. I hope he's not interfering with next door's whippet again. That animal's been through enough.

JUAN: Beautiful lady.

MRS HORROCKS: All right, so what are you flogging?

JUAN: Let us not talk of flagellation on a day such as this.

MRS HORROCKS: What day?

JUAN: The day when the gods of love smiled down on us. The day when our destinies are fulfilled. The day when I drowned in your eyes for the first time. Take of me what you desire. I can please you like no other man you've known.

MRS HORROCKS: I don't like 'em too stringy.

JUAN: I won't disappoint you.

MRS HORROCKS: Hold your 'orses. I'm not saying yes 'till I've had a good feel.

JUAN: I've never had any complaints.

MRS HORROCKS: Get 'em out, then.

JUAN: Just like that. Perhaps we draw the blinds?

MRS HORROCKS: I thought you was selling onions, not raising the dead.

JUAN: I'm not an onion seller!

MRS HORROCKS: Well then, you'd best be off. You could be up to all kinds of shenanigans here in the master's study.

JUAN: Don't deny it.

MRS HORROCKS: Don't deny what?

JUAN: That stirring in your bosom.

MRS HORROCKS: Listen sunshine, nothing's stirred in this bosom since a flutter of girlish pride last coronation day.

The Latin Love Train

JUAN: (*Sings.*) Cruel seductress, you break my heart
You flash those eyes and the music starts.
Can't you hear it from paradise?
It's oh so naughty, but oh so nice.
Hear the rhythm of Latin Love
A little gift from the gods above.
Just give into it's heady beat
Stir your passions and move your feet
(*JUAN adds the* l'amour *response, whilst MRS HORROCKS sings.*)

MRS HORROCKS: Something's happ'ning, I'd best sit down
    Why is the room spinning round and round?
    The desk needs dusting, can't hang about
    Must feed the cat, get the Hoover out.

JUAN: Just toss your head
    Forget regrets
    And click your fingers
    Like they're castanets.
    Then sway your hips
    From side to side
    I am your love train
    Baby, take a ride.

MRS HORROCKS: You filthy beast!

JUAN: It's up to you,
    There's so much dancing
    Left for us to do.

MRS HORROCKS: Just sling your hook.

JUAN: Well then goodbye,
    Each time I think of what we've
    (*Hang on to next note.*) Lo-ost I'll die.
    (*He is overcome with grief. She tries to placate him.*)

MRS HORROCKS: Now don't take on
    You're very sweet
    It's been a while since
    I had dancing feet
    Perhaps I'll have a little sway
    I used to like to
    (*Mispronounced with extra syllable.*) Pasedobalay.

JUAN: You drive me wild

MRS HORROCKS: You've made me blush
    Savour the moment
    There's no need to rush.
    (*JUAN, unobserved, looks at his watch.*)

JUAN: I want you now

MRS HORROCKS: Don't be absurd.
    I feel all funny,
    Ooh I say, my word!
    (*They dance.*)

JUAN: That's more like it. You're doing good.

MRS HORROCKS: I rather like this

JUAN: I knew you would

MRS HORROCKS: In my mind you're a matador

JUAN: My little bull, glide across the floor.

MRS HORROCKS: Her next door ought to see me now
    She'd have a seizure, the snotty cow.

JUAN: Just relax, let your passions fly

MRS HORROCKS: I'll be the Carmen of the WI.
    (*Now MRS HORROCKS sings the* l'amour*s*.)

MRS HORROCKS: (*Spoken.*) Ooh Mr…?

JUAN: (*Spoken.*) Call me Juan.

MRS HORROCKS: (*Sung.*) L'amour. (*Spoken.*) Juan what?

JUAN: (*Spoken.*) I have many names.

MRS HORROCKS: L'amour (*etc..*)

JUAN: Juan's in a life time
    Juan singular sensation
    Juan's a night is not enough

BOTH: Just toss your head
    Forget regrets
    And click your fingers
    Like they're castanets
    Then sway your hips
    From side to side
    (*Big finish.*) I am your love train
    Baby, take a ride.

MRS HORROCKS: Will you excuse me a moment, while I
    slip into something a little more comfortable?

JUAN: A sexy negligee?

MRS HORROCKS: No, me orthopedic slippers.
    This dancing's playing merry hell with me corns.

JUAN: Of course, my angel.

MRS HORROCKS: Would you like me to pop the wireless
    on for you? Ooh look, I think its time for 'The Organist
    Entertains'.
    (*He goes crazy.*)

JUAN: No! No! NO! I hate it! Never mention it again in my
    presence! It holds terrible memories for me!

MRS HORROCKS: I know what you mean. There's only so

many times you can tap along to 'I Do Like to Be Beside the Seaside', isn't there? (*She goes.*)

JUAN: (*Speaking into his wrist watch.*) Love Thug to HQ. Alright, I'm alone in Barton's study. Just putting the bomb in position now. (*He places the bomb in a vase which he leaves on the desk.*) Our boffins have programmed it to detonate when my signature tune is sung within its vicinity. I'll pick my moment and then whistle it down the dog and bone.

DICK BARTON: (*Off.*) Snowy, for heaven sake, will you stop making that wailing sound. Are you in pain?

JUAN: Someone's coming. I'd better get out of here sharpish. There's a drain pipe. (*He climbs out of the window.*)

(*BARTON and SNOWY enter.*)

DICK BARTON: Ever since we left the cricket ground, you've been gesticulating wildly and making the most extraordinary noises.

SNOWY: I'm trying to crack a secret code.

DICK BARTON: Now look here, Snowy, you've been told about this before. Leave the clever stuff to us public school chaps. Honest strong armed thuggery is your department.

SNOWY: Sorry Guv, but I thought you'd be cross with me.

DICK BARTON: My dear fellow. Why should I be cross?

SNOWY: 'Cos I've made a right cock up of things. Secret Agent Rodger gave me a secret code tune to remember which identifies an international terrorist who's after the whereabouts of our secret agents around the world, and who they reckon is going to try and bump us off.

DICK BARTON: Is that all, you silly old sausage. Just hum us a few bars and we'll clear the matter up in no time. (*SNOWY sings tunelessly.*)

How strange, I believe that's the call to prayer of Matowby tribesman.

SNOWY: Umm. It might not be.

DICK BARTON: What do you mean, old fellow?

SNOWY: All right. This is me singing the code tune (*Unrecognisable wail.*) and this is me singing the hit tune from *Do It Daisy Do* at The Adelphi (*Another.*) and this is me singing 'Happy Birthday To You'. (*Another.*)

DICK BARTON: But they're exactly the same.

SNOWY: I know. I can never remember tunes when someone's listening. It comes out all mangled. But if I can't sing it to you, how are you going to recognise it when those same notes signal danger?

DICK BARTON: You've probably got the wrong end of the stick old fellow.

(*The phone rings.*

JUAN in a phone box.)

JUAN: Just a few notes down the phone and you'll be blown to smithereens Barton.

(*BARTON picks up the phone leaning very close to the vase.*)

DICK BARTON: (*Without waiting to hear JUAN speak.*) I say would you mind awfully calling back a little bit later. We're rather busy at the moment. (*He puts the receiver down.*)

JUAN: Curses!

DICK BARTON: Secret code tunes. Really Snowy! Have you been at the John Buchan again?

SNOWY: It's what Mr Rodger told me.

DICK BARTON: I'll simply give him a ring at his Earls Court *pied à terre* and find out myself.

(*As he dials, MRS HORROCKS bursts in. She is in a sexy negligé. She has her hair down and a flower in it.*)

MRS HORROCKS: It's only me, my little conquistador.

(*The boys don't bat an eyelid.*)

DICK BARTON: Ah, Mrs Horrocks. There'll be one less for tea tonight. Jock's off on one of his jaunts. There's something different about you, isn't there? Don't tell me. Let me guess. You've taken my advice and shaved your upper lip. Good show. Close the door on your way out.

MRS HORROCKS: Men! (*She strops out.*)

DICK BARTON: (*With the phone.*) Odd, I'm not getting any answer. He and Wilco must be away on a mission.

SNOWY: You don't suppose something's happened to them, do you?

DICK BARTON: Nonsense. Foreign skullduggery is no
   match for a member of British intelligence.
   (*The phone rings again. DICK BARTON leans past the vase
   to pick it up.*)
   Not now! (*Puts the phone down.*) Funny! Sort of whistling
   noise in the receiver. Must ask the post office to test the
   line. No, Snowy old man, I'm sure there's a perfectly
   rational explanation for all this.

SPECIAL AGENT COOL
(*Sings.*) If one thing has inspired me
Through Barton family history
It's our impressive mastery
Of keeping a cool head.
In an emergency
We've always done things stoic'lly
For flapping in a panic
Might have meant a Barton dead.

Great grandfather Barton's cat
Was very quick at spotting that
One dreadful night the feline
Was pursued by vicious hounds.
Threatened by this grim event
He lured then through some wet cement.
The milkman found them stuck there
On his early morning rounds.

(*Tune segues into 'Daisy, Daisy'.*)
Uncle Cuthburt
Led us at Katmandu.
Under siege he pondered what he should do.
His starving troops were manic
But he knew not to panic
He quickly cooked a raw recruit
In a nourishing, Irish stew.

(*Back to Red Indian style arrangement of 'Early One Morning'.*)
Intrepid Great Aunt Guenivere

Was a Wild West frontier pioneer,
Imagine her distraction
As an Indian appears.
With celebrated Barton pluck
She spoke with Big Chief Sitting Duck
And now they run a gift shop
Selling native souvenirs.

The moral of this song is plain
When trouble rears its head again
Don't let rash decisions
Make you look a bally fool.
Faced with almost certain death
Just take a big deep Barton breath
And never, never, ever loose
Your special agent cool
(*DICK BARTON and SNOWY slow it right down for a big finish.*)
No, never, never ever loose
Your special agent –
(*COLONEL GARDENER bursts in.*)

COLONEL GARDENER: Oh my god! Oh my God! It's a disaster! What are we going to do?

DICK BARTON/SNOWY: (*Sung.*) – *Cool!*

DICK BARTON: Steady on there, Colonel Gardener. It looks like you need a calming cup of tea. Why don't I ask Mrs Horrocks if she can rustle you up some hot buttered muffins?

COLONEL GARDENER: There's no time for that now. Two of Britain's finest secret agents and Judy Garland experts are in mortal danger.

DICK BARTON: Rodger and Wilco?

COLONEL GARDENER: Quite so. The dossier containing their latest undercover identity has been stolen by an agent of EFIL. Miss Thrupnybit from the typing pool was transferring the document from the filing cabinet with the coffee stain, to the one with the Aspidistra on the top, when her attention was drawn to the window. In a Whitehall street, a greasy foreign Johnny was serenading her with some kind of Latino love song. Naturally the poor gal was torn between instigating emergency alert 39.5, subsection code 6 –

DICK BARTON: Screaming loudly?

COLONEL GARDENER: – Quite – or taking up the foreigner's offer of a night of passion in the back row of the Gaumont Cinema. She naturally chose –

SNOWY: The Gaumont.

COLONEL GARDENER: Precisely. The devils know it's our weakness. They get us with it every time. The fellow was rushing her so they could catch the 6.20 showing of *Playtime in Pall Mall*, and so she took the dossier with her. After the cad had had his wicked way with her, she discovered the file had gone. Needless to say so had her seducer. And now EFIL will know the secret location of Rodger and Wilco.

DICK BARTON: Presumably they're in a high-risk scenario.

COLONEL GARDENER: Of course. After you, Barton, they're our bravest men. Tireless chappies, you don't find them moaning on about taking time off to visit their wives. At present, they're investigating an international corned beef cartel, disguised as Argentinian tango instructors at the Tippy Toe Dance Academy, Buenos Aires. (*Horror.*) Unless an agent of EFIL has already got to them.

DICK BARTON: You've warned them, of course?

COLONEL GARDENER: Too risky. If we let EFIL know we're on to them, they'll have a couple of hit men round to our boys in a second. Our only hope is that they bide their time hoping to get all the files on all the agents before launching a concentrated attack on all our people around the world. They won't succeed of course. All the other files are locked in this briefcase and I've handcuffed it to my wrist. It's not going anywhere. You, on the other hand Barton, must go to Buenos Aires and warn Rodger and Wilco.

DICK BARTON: I've a spare trilby and macintosh packed for just such an emergency.

COLONEL GARDENER: Good man. We've booked you on to the next flight to Argentina, first thing in the morning.

DICK BARTON: Understood Colonel. Don't worry about a thing. Barton's on the case.

COLONEL GARDENER: Jolly good. Well, I'll leave you to make arrangements. Sleep well, and remember serious crime is a lot rarer than you think, don't have nightmares.

DICK BARTON: Goodnight, Colonel.

(*The COLONEL leaves.*)

SNOWY: Blimey, I feel terrible. If only I'd been able to think of that song, I could have warned that poor girl at the Ministry.

DICK BARTON: No point crying over spilt milk now, old fellow. You and Jock will need all the initiative you can muster if you're to hold the fort whilst I'm away.

SNOWY: You've got nothing to worry about there, Guv.

DICK BARTON: I know, Snowy.

SNOWY: Guv?

DICK BARTON: Yes, Snowy.

SNOWY: What's does 'dossier' mean again?

(*Blackout. A phone rings.*)

Scene 4

A Spanish restaurant in South London.

JUAN answers the phone.

JUAN: (*Latino accent.*) Tapas Temptations, the Old Kent Road. Table for two? Eight o'clock. Certainly, señor.
(*He hangs up, writes down the reservation then calls into the kitchen.*)
(*Cockney accent.*) You can forget it, Mamma. I'm sorry Uncle Pedro's off sick, but you're not getting me working in the family restaurant again. I've told you before, I'm a dangerous international anarchist, gigolo and jewel thief now. I've got a dastardly foreign plot to sort out.

(*From the kitchen off we hear a formidable sounding woman swearing in Spanish and throwing pots around. JUAN winces. He speaks into his watch again.*)

(*Latino accent.*) Love Thug to HQ. I need you to get an urgent message to our boy Diego, first bongo player in the BBC's Mambo Combo. You'll find him in rehearsals at Broadcasting House for *Friday Night is Music Night.* Tell him I need them to perform a request. I want them to play my signature tune over the air at the top of tonight's show. It's a coded tune that will detonate a bomb at Barton HQ. That's all. No, wait… there's a dedication. To Mrs Edna Horrocks of Wimpole Street. Hope you and your boss hear this loud and clear. A little something to remember me by… Or something like that.

(*A shifty-looking STRANGER enters.*

JUAN calls into the kitchen.)

Mamma you've got a customer!

(*No response. He sighs and continues.*)

Good evening señor, smoking or non-smoking?

STRANGER: (*Foreign accent.*) Neither. I too, am a member of Evil Foreigners In London.

(*They exchange the EFIL salute.*)

I am come to warn you that the scotch sidekick of Richard Barton is heading this way.

JUAN: (*Cockney accent.*) Excellent. Barton and me old mate, Snowy, are set to be blown apart with a little help from the BBC's Mambo Minstrels. Plus, I've got time to put a bullet through this tartan ninny's head and still reach Whitehall to nick the rest of the files.

STRANGER: Our leaders are very pleased with you.

JUAN: Just you make sure they know I'm only in this for the diamonds, and to avenge my family honour.

STRANGER: Family honour?

JUAN: I'll teach the scum a lesson. Pappa won't have died in vain

STRANGER: In Spain?

JUAN: I said 'vain'. It's a terrible story of thwarted ambition and the shattered dreams of what might have been…

SETTLING SCORES
(*Sings.*) Dad played his organ
At the cinema.
It was quite an organ
Made him a star.
One day he wrote a
Very special song
(*Sings The Tune.*)
Anyone who's learnt it
Never gets it wrong.

You didn't need to save any fees
For piano lessons to play the keys
He didn't think to
Copyright his work
So everybody pinched it
What a jerk.

That's when I learnt that smart guys
Usually win the race.
So I became a bad 'un
Cruel, with a pretty face.
Shamelessly I'm a bastard
I've found it opens doors
It's ever so satisfying
Settling your scores.

Soon everyone was
Banging out pa's tune.
'Cause he'd performed it
Too bloody soon.
If he had only waited
Had a patent there
He'd have been a multi-Millionaire.
I will avenge him, soon they will pay
Wake up and shiver, it's judgment day.
They'll learn to fear that melody he wrote
The tune that they stole will
Stick in their throat

Father you showed me nice guys
Usually finish last
You're why I'm such a rotter
With a shady past.
Shamelessly, I'm a bastard
I find it opens doors
But don't you worry Pa, I'm
Settling your scores.

(*Spoken.*) Ma wanted a life of luxury dripping in diamonds, not the love of a lowly cinema organist who'd thrown away his one big chance. She chucked him out and started this pioneering Old Kent Road Tapas Bar. He wandered the streets deranged with frustration and remorse, whistling his tune to whoever would listen. The night he died in my arms at that Lewisham asylum, with his last gasp he sang it to the blood red moon. And I vowed to make it my anthem until all the world suffered as he had. Vengeance is why I toil tirelessly for EFIL.

STRANGER: I know what you mean, they pay us rubbish.

JUAN: 'Ere, you don't want to make few extra bob, do you?

STRANGER: (*With relish.*) Is it a dirty job?

JUAN: Stinking! Get a cloth from out the back and start wiping these tables down. We've got a hen night booked in for seven. Don't mess up the orders.

(*The STRANGER exits to the kitchen.*

JOCK enters the restaurant. JUAN ducks down behind the counter.)

JOCK: (*Looking around.*) Hello, my Spanish friends. Is anybody there? I wonder if someone could help me with an investigation? I'm looking for a swarthy-looking laddie who might be flogging some jewellery he's nicked off a lady friend of mine.

(*No response. JOCK has an idea. He calls out.*)

Oh, uno momento. (*He takes out a Spanish phrase book and repeats what he's just said, with a bad Spanish accent.*) Eello, my espaniol amigos. Is anybody there? I wonder if someone could help me with an investigation?

(*He has his back to the counter to consult the phrase book.*
As he does so JUAN rises from behind the counter with a gun.)
I'm looking for a swarthy-looking laddie who might be
flogging some jewellery he's nicked off a lady friend of
mine.

JUAN: Goodbye forever, you meddlesome Scot.
(*But just as he is about to pull the trigger, DAPHNE bursts in.*
JUAN ducks behind the counter again.)

JOCK: Daphne!

DAPHNE: Jock!

JOCK: What on earth are you doing here?

DAPHNE: Oh Jock, I...I...I followed you here. I couldn't
bare to think my foolishness had put you in any danger.
Perhaps now, I realise that my feelings for you run a
little deeper then girlish friendship.

JOCK: Oh Lassie, you don't know how glad I am to hear
that.
(*JUAN grabs his coat and sneaks out.*)

DAPHNE: Oh cruel world, that has placed such obstacles
in the path of our true love.
(*The restaurant door clangs shut.*)

JOCK: What was that?

DAPHNE: Other people. Someone else trying to come
between us.

JOCK: Och, why can't they leave us alone. Oh, Daphne, do
you know what I dream sometimes? It's just a silly wee
fancy but...

DAPHNE: Tell me, Jock. What's your dream?

JOCK: Just you and I, in a little council house in the
Gorbals. A dozen wee bairns running around your feet,
their bonny tear-stained faces gazing up at you, as you
lovingly comb the nits out of their hair. And me, rolling
in at midnight, to give you all a big sloppy kiss after a
skinful down the pub.

DAPHNE: (*Breathlessly romantic.*) And would we have a tin
bath and an outdoor convenience?

JOCK: Of course we would, lassie.

DAPHNE: Oh Jock, will we ever know such happiness?

JOCK: Daphne! I won't let you down. I promise. I'll get your jewellery back and no one will keep us apart.

DAPHNE: My hero!

BBC ANNOUNCER: (*Moved.*) D'you know, it puts me in mind of when I met my Angela. Sometimes her halitosis made us feel like it was us against the world. (*Pulls himself together.*) Meanwhile, back at Barton HQ, our hero little suspects he's sat on top of a time bomb, as he briefs the trusty Mrs Horrocks on domestic arrangements.

Scene 5

DICK BARTON's HQ.

DICK BARTON is in his dressing gown.

DICK BARTON: Could I have lightly boiled egg in the morning, Mrs H? That should keep me going on the long flight.

MRS HORROCKS: (*In floods of tears.*) Yes sir, lightly boiled, sir.

DICK BARTON: I don't know how I'm going to manage to avoid all that foreign food. They do say one taste of foreign and you're hooked.

(*MRS HORROCKS wails.*)

Mrs Horrocks, whatever is the matter? You've been blubbing all morning. Have I said something to upset you?

MRS HORROCKS: No sir, it's not you sir. I've had my heart broken, cruelly ripped apart by a smooth talking, broad shouldered, slim-hipped brute.

DICK BARTON: (*Distracted.*) I say. Oh and by the way could I have two rounds of soldiers with my egg? In this life you just can't be sure the next time you're going to get any.

(*MRS HORROCKS wails.*)

MRS HORROCKS: You've never said a truer word, sir.

DICK BARTON: Well look, chin up. It's nearly time for your favourite programme, *Friday Night Is Music Night.*

MRS HORROCKS: Oh, Mr Barton, I've taken no pleasure at all in the wireless since you told me the BBC has been infiltrated by communists.

DICK BARTON: Don't worry, Mrs H, that's all sorted. Only Cambridge men in charge now.

MRS HORROCKS: That's a mercy indeed. Shall I bring your cocoa to you in your bath as usual, sir?

DICK BARTON: Thank you, yes. I think Snowy's taking his in the garage, fitting some new gadget for the Bentley.

MRS HORROCKS: Rightie ho, Mr Barton.

(*DICK BARTON exits to his bath, MRS HORROCKS to the kitchen, turning on the wireless as she leaves. The sound of tuning, then we see a lady PRESENTER. She is 1950s glam and very slick: Angela Rippon on 'Come Dancing' or Katie Boyle doing the 'Eurovision Song Contest'.*)

PRESENTER: Good evening every one, and welcome to *Friday Night Is Music Night.* And it's quite a line up we've got for you this evening. Coming up, we've got Britain's answer to the sharp-witted comedy genius of Bob Hope, cuddly Arthur Askey, with a smashing new song about a busy little bee.

(*Clapping and laughter. MRS HORROCKS takes DICK BARTON his cocoa through and returns to dust as she listens.*)

My word, isn't he a caution. Later on we're pushing back the boundaries of wirelesses light entertainment with radio's first plate spinning demonstration. But first of all, let's get a little Latin.

(*MRS HORROCKS sobs.*)

Yes, it's Murray Micklethrope and his merry mob of Mambo Minstrels. But what's this? Little Diego, the drummer is handing me a piece of paper. I wonder if... Yes it is, it's a dedication. I wonder who the lucky señorita can be.

(*MRS HORROCKS picks up the vase containing the bomb to dust it.*)

This song goes out to Mrs Edna Horrocks.

(*MRS HORROCKS freezes.*)

From your little love bunny, Juan. (*She carries the booby-trapped vase over to the wireless.*)

He says thanks for the crumpet – be seeing you around. And here's tonight's big, big number to remember him by…

BBC ANNOUNCER: What will happen? Is this the thin end of the wedge? Will they be letting girls read the news next? Will the musical code in the mambo tune mean it's ba-da-boom-bye-bye-Barton? Or will there still be eggy soldiers in the morning? Are Rodger and Wilco safe? Can Jock return Daphne's jewels and save her reputation? Will Mrs Horrocks ever find true love again? And how did Arthur Askey get away with it for so long? Some, if not all, of these questions will be answered after the interval, in the next exciting instalment of – Dick Barton, Special Agent!

End of Act One.

ACT TWO

BBC ANNOUNCER: Welcome back. If you were paying attention before the break you'll know that we're at a very exciting point in our story. If however your mind was wandering in anticipation of your interval gin and tonic, here's a quick recap. A Fiendish Latin Lothario with an eye for the ladies, and light fingers for their jewellery, has been hired by the forces of EFIL to swipe secret files detailing the whereabouts of British secret agents. Ruthless foreigners are waiting to pounce on our boys including Britain's finest, Secret Agents Rodger and Wilco, currently undercover in Argentina. Dick Barton's sidekick, Jock Anderson, is on a mission to save the honour of the lovely Daphne Fritters, whose jewellery has been stolen by the swarthy devil. Meanwhile, Dick Barton's efforts to foil the foreigner's plot have been hampered by the inability of his other loveable working class assistant, Snowy White, to remember a code tune identifying the enemy agent. The same tune indeed, which will now cause a bomb to detonate as it's heard across the airwaves in *Friday Night is Music Night.* And perhaps, most extraordinary of all, the programme is being presented by a girl. Got all that? Good. We go now to Broadcasting house where the talentless floozy is addressing the nation.

Scene 1

A studio at Broadcasting House.

The lady PRESENTER is at a microphone centre stage.

PRESENTER: Little Diego, the drummer, has handed me a piece of paper. I wonder if…yes it is, it's a dedication. I wonder who the lucky senorita can be. This song goes out to Mrs Edna Horrocks. From your little love bunny Juan. He says thanks for the crumpet – be seeing you around. So here's tonight's big, big number to remember him by.

(*DICK BARTON enters wearing a towel, with a loofer and covered in foam as if from the bath.*)

DICK BARTON: Stop right there. The future of the free world is at stake.

PRESENTER: My goodness me listeners, we've an unscheduled guest in the studio. Great heavens, it's Special Agent and tea time wireless celebrity, Dick Barton.

DICK BARTON: I'm sorry to interrupt the fun, listeners. (*To the PRESENTER.*) I hope I didn't startle you, Genevieve.

GENEVIEVE: It's a pleasure to have you on the show, Dick. But my goodness, you look as if you've been taking a bath.

DICK BARTON: That's exactly what I wanted everyone to think. You see, I had to let the forces of EFIL think I'd let my guard down, but I knew there was mischief a foot. A few weeks ago, my black market informants told me that a shifty looking foreigner had been making enquiries about a Quantum, electri-audio meticululator. You're a girl so I don't expect that'll mean anything to you.

(*GENEVIEVE smiles.*)

It's a piece of bomb-making equipment used to recognise impulses generated by any given configuration of beats. It can be programmed to detonate a bomb at a certain Morse Code sequence for instance, or when a prearranged tune is played in its vicinity.

(*Again GENEVIEVE smiles.*)

When I heard that there was an enemy agent in town with his own distinctive signature tune, I knew it wouldn't be long before vanity led him to use it as a cue for mischief. A glance at the *Radio Times* told me that tonight's program opened with a foreign swing combo, so I climbed out of the bathroom window, leaving a decoy in the bubbles, and here I am. Just in time to stop you broadcasting a tune that could detonate an explosion somewhere in London.

FLOOR MANAGER: The Mambo group have legged it and taken their sheet music with them. And Arthur Askey's locked himself in the karzy again. I've got some musicians from Animal Playtime to stand in until we can talk him out of there.

DICK BARTON: I'd better get after those Latin Rhythm junkies or we'll never know what the secret code tune is. Good night, everyone.

GENEVIEVE: Just a minute! You're not leaving me with five minutes of empty airtime to fill. (*Into the microphone.*) Exciting news everybody! Dick Barton has just agreed to join me and the Animal Playtime band in a little song.

DICK BARTON: Madame, I really don't think... I'm one of His Majesty's special agents on a mission of international importance that could save the free world.

GENEVIEVE: (*To the band.*) Hit it!

> I LIKE-A-YOU
> (*Sings.*) Oh darling we're the perfect fit
> Why don't you loosen up a bit

DICK BARTON: I'd love to stay and sing this hit
(*He notices an escaping Mambo musician in a sombrero sneaking out with an instrument.*)
> But while we're japing
> EFIL's escaping
> (*GENEVIEVE jerks BARTON round to face the front.*)

LADY PRESENTER: You wrecked my show! I'm growing
>   tired
> It was a fight to get me hired
> I'll kill you if you've got me fired
> Just shut right up and sing –

BOTH: If you lak-a-me
> Lak I lak-a-you
> And we lak-a both the same

DICK BARTON:
> I lak-a say
> This very day
> I lak-a change your name

BOTH: Cause I love a-you
>And love a-you true
>And if you a-love a me
>One live as two
>Two live as one
>Under the bamboo tree!
>(*DICK BARTON notices another musician in a sombrero with an instrument sneaking out.*)

GENEVIEVE: And when the jungle starts to sway
>We'll woo each other every day

DICK BARTON: (*Trying to pursue the musician.*)
>I think I'd best be on my way.

GENEVIEVE: (*Yanking him back.*)
>You leave me dang'ling
>You'll get a mang'ling!
>So here beneath the bamboo green
>Make me your Mambo Bamboo queen;
>Oh what a happy jungle scene
>Let's sing out our song:
>(*A stream of Mexican musicians escape during the following.*)

BOTH: If you lak-a-me
>Lak I lak-a-you
>And we lak-a both the same
>I lak-a say
>This very day
>I lak-a change your name

>Cause I love a-you
>And love a-you true
>And if you a-love a me
>One live as two
>Two live as one
>Under the bamboo tree!

DICK BARTON: (*Spoken.*) Can I go now?
>(*GENEVIEVE looks to the wings.*)

STUDIO MANAGER: (*Off.*) Arthur says he needs a couple more minutes.

GENEVIEVE: Big finish!
>(*The tune goes into raunchy half-time swing.*)

This little story, strange but true,
Is often told in Mataboo
Of how this Zulu tried to woo
DICK BARTON: His jungle lady
GENEVIEVE: In tropics shady
DICK BARTON: Although the scene was miles away
Right here at home I dare to say
GENEVIEVE: You'll hear some Zulu every day
BOTH: Gush out this soft refrain:
If you lak-a-me
Lak I lak-a-you
And we lak-a both the same
I lak-a say
This very day
I lak-a change your name

Cause I love a-you
And love a-you true
And if you a-love a me
One live as two
Two live as one
Under the bamboo tree!
BBC ANNOUNCER: I knew there'd be trouble. They'll be
letting women spin the hit parade next. Some hours later
at Barton HQ, Colonel Gardener and Mrs Horrocks wait
anxiously for the special agent's return.

Scene 2

DICK BARTON's HQ.

COLONEL GARDENER pacing. MRS HORROCKS on the phone.

MRS HORROCKS: Yes, I'll tell him. As soon as he gets in.
Yes. (*She puts the phone down.*)
COLONEL GARDENER: Who was that?
MRS HORROCKS: The BBC again. They want to release
Mr Barton's duet with that wireless lady as a single.
Apparently pre-sales have already gone platinum in
Scandinavia.

COLONEL GARDENER: What can be keeping him? He's going to miss that plane to Argentina.

MRS HORROCKS: He's got to find out where the bomb is hidden. Someone would only have to whistle a few bars of that coded tune and there'll be a huge explosion somewhere.

COLONEL GARDENER: I am aware of that, Madam.

MRS HORROCKS: 'Scuse me talking out of turn Sir, I'm all worn out. It was quite a shock I can tell you finding that stand in for Mr Barton in the bathtub. Still, he had lovely manners though, and you couldn't fault his personal hygiene – very thorough. It's funny, five hours ago I thought my heart would break in two, now I quite fancy an egg sandwich and a couple of pickled onions. Onions! (*She starts to cry again.*)

COLONEL GARDENER: For heaven sake, woman, don't start that again. You certainly wouldn't find me trusting my heart to a foreigner.

MRS HORROCKS: If only I had your common sense, Colonel. Why don't you put that briefcase down? It looks very heavy.

COLONEL GARDENER: Indeed it is, Mrs Horrocks, for it contains weighty matters indeed. In this case are the secret whereabouts of all of Britain's secret agents. Since the location of Rodger and Wilco was stolen, I'm taking no chances and keeping it handcuffed to my wrist until the danger is over.

MRS HORROCKS: Very brave, I'm sure.
(*SNOWY and JOCK enter. JOCK is intently reading a phrase book.*)

SNOWY: Alright mateys? The governor back yet?

COLONEL GARDENER: No, he's not, and what are you two doing lounging around here? Can't you get out on the streets and find some clues or something.

SNOWY: Well, I'm game, but I don't reckon you'll get old Jock's head out of that 'learn to speak foreign' book. Says he's researching a case of his own.

JOCK: (*Reads aloud a Spanish phrase and then translates it as.*)
'Where is the Jewellery? Your mother is a whore and
your father makes love to his donkey.'

COLONEL GARDENER: (*Sharply.*) Anderson!
(*JOCK looks up.*)
I want you to stop what ever it is you're doing and
concentrate on the operation in hand, is that clear?

JOCK: Och, but I'm sorry Colonel. I can't leave this now.
I've got a very important case to solve.

COLONEL GARDENER: It's an order Anderson. I want
you to get out there and try and track down these ghastly
criminals. You'll provide me with an hourly report on
your efforts, and I don't want to hear of you getting
distracted again. Anyway, what can you possibly be up
to that's more important then the safety of our boys
overseas.

JOCK: Well you see, it's a matter of *l'amour.*

COLONEL GARDENER: Of what?

MRS HORROCKS: *L'amour.* (*She wails again.*)

COLONEL GARDENER: You're jeopardising a top
priority assignment to cannoodle with a sweetheart?

JOCK: Oh, but if you could only see the look in her eyes.
She really loves me this time. It's just we've got to clear
up the little matter of her letting a Spaniard whip her
jewellery.

MRS HORROCKS: Oh, the poor love. I know what she's
going through. You let your defences down for a minute
and those greasy devils'll have your gusset all of a
tangle.

COLONEL GARDENER: What is the matter with you,
woman? What's wrong with an honest stout-hearted
British Romeo?

SNOWY: (*Belches.*) Better out than in.

COLONEL GARDENER: No wonder they say British
Intelligence is an oxymoron.

SNOWY: I've always said it.

COLONEL GARDENER: Don't start!

JOCK: Colonel Gardener, sir.

COLONEL GARDENER: What is it now, man?

JOCK: Can I have permission to telephone my lassie and tell her that I've got to put things on hold for a while?

COLONEL GARDENER: I suppose so. But be sharp about it. Well, I've got better things to do then sit around gassing with you love sick young pups. Tell Barton to call me at Whitehall.

MRS HORROCKS: We certainly will, sir.

COLONEL: Good night to you all. (*He leaves.*)

MRS HORROCKS: Come along, Snowy. I think our Jock wants to some privacy.

SNOWY: Why? Is he going to put that ointment on again?

MRS HORROCKS: (*Sharp.*) Kitchen now!

> (*SNOWY goes.*)
> (*To JOCK, very Anna from* The King and I.) I too have known what it is to love.

> THE CALL
> Can you feel it call you?
> Romance is in the air
> Time to pluck my eyebrows
> And dye some blue rinse into my hair.
> When romance is calling
> The floor wax smells so sweet
> And my Linoleum buffs up a treat.

JOCK: Och, I know that feeling
> The Porridge has nee lumps
> You can smell the heather
> You toss the caber. Your heart fairly jumps.
> When romance is calling
> Why even Nessie sings,
> And you've an urge to dance ten highland flings.
> (*We catch a glimpse of DICK BARTON out and about, looking for clues.*)

DICK BARTON: Can you feel it call you?
> Adventures in the air
> Breathe in raw adrenalin
> Many men have been caught in the snare.
> When adventure's calling

It's time to face your foe
Pack some egg sandwiches and off you go!
MRS HORROCKS: But beware the call for the human
                                                heart can break.
DICK BARTON: One wrong move can blow it
    The freedom of the world is at stake.
MRS HORROCKS/JOCK: Love is like adventure
    Whichever path you choose
    There's much to gain but such pain if you lose.

BBC ANNOUNCER: Ah, why does the course of true love
    never run smooth? One of the great universal mysteries
    that has troubled the great thinkers down the centuries.
    Is there life after death? Are we working through some
    preordained fate or are our lives just a tragic, comic
    ragbag of coincidences? And why does one always loose
    one's umbrella on public transport? But we must put
    such lofty thoughts aside now, as we cross to Whitehall
    where Colonel Gardener, with his briefcase still
    handcuffed to his wrist, is awaiting news from Dick
    Barton as to the whereabouts of the musically activated
    bomb.

Scene 3

COLONEL GARDENER's office.

COLONEL GARDENER: Reginald Hilary Gardener. This
    could be your Agincourt. When they see my portrait in
    the MI5 hall of fame, they'll say, wasn't he in charge that
    autumn? The autumn of the Tango of Terror? Yes, this is
    the big one. No one is going to remember that
    unfortunate incident with the grenadier guard, the
    whippet and the half a pound of Brussel sprouts, after
    this. And to think Father said I wouldn't amount to
    anything. Father, the 'brilliant military strategist'! Well,
    he'd never think of handcuffing himself to an attaché
    case, would he? So, who's the clever one now, eh, father
    dearest. Those foreigners will never get their greasy

hands on this! Even if they did, what use will it be. Only I know the combination and no one's going to make me squeal.

(*The phone rings.*)

Miss Thrupnybit? What on earth are you doing back here at this hour? Someone to see me? But it's the middle of the night. I don't want a big surprise. Oh very well, show him in. (*He hangs up.*) Curious.

(*From outside we hear someone whistling. It is JUAN.*)

Well, jaunty sort of fellow whoever he is.

(*A knock at the door.*)

Enter.

BBC ANNOUNCER: At that very moment, Dick and Jock climb into the Barton Bentley, intent on making their way through the dark empty streets of midnight London to the Colonel's office.

Scene 4

In the Barton Bentley.

BARTON is studying a map.

JOCK: Do you think Mrs Horrocks will be alright, DB?

DICK BARTON: No question about it. Snowy's there to make sure she's in good spirits.

JOCK: That's what I'm afraid of.

DICK BARTON: Have no fear on that account. I've hidden the gin under the commode. We all need to keep a clear head. Now, the mysterious woman at the Brazilian opium den I discovered just off Kensal Rise, gave me a clue as to where the bomb is hidden. But I can't make head nor tail of it. Curse her and her drug-crazed riddles.

JOCK: Well why don't you tell me, DB? I might be able to help untangle the hellish muddle.

DICK BARTON: I'd love to Jock, but you know what Home Office rules say about not exposing the lower ranks to thinking.

JOCK: Aye, I suppose you're right. I just thought it might while away the journey to Whitehall.

DICK BARTON: And so it shall! Well then, what do you make of this fiendish conundrum, my merry buccaneer? When I asked the wretched hag what she could tell me of the bomb's whereabouts, a strange look came into her eye and she said this: 'Be it ever so humble, there's no place like *boom*!' and then cackling, she disappeared into the foul-smelling vapours where I dared not follow.

JOCK: Och, that's a teaser and no mistake.

DICK BARTON: Don't let it get you down, old chap, or they really will have us beaten.

JOCK: Plaice? Humble? Could it mean an understated fish shop? Och, my head's reeling just thinking about it.

DICK BARTON: Not to worry. The Colonel and I will set our old grey matter to work. I've asked HQ to have the phrase analysed phonetically in a number of different Brazilian dialects. We can then cross-refer the speech patterns with the coded rhythms our fellows have been picking up in enemy territory.

JOCK: Very impressive, DB. But what if the answer's closer to home?

DICK BARTON: I'm afraid we can't think like that, Jock old boy. Whitehall regulations are very clear about never underestimating foreign fiendishness. Ah, here we are at Whitehall. Pull into Winston's parking space, I'm sure he won't mind.

BBC ANNOUNCER: In this dark hour, the two took some comfort in knowing the Bentley was safely stowed where the war time prime minister had so often entrusted his staff car. But what a scene of unimaginable horror was to greet our heroes in Colonel Gardener's office.

Scene 5

COLONEL GARDENER's office.

COLONEL GARDENER is sat in his chair, his hands cuffed behind his back, wearing a matador's jacket open over a bare chest, 'TOP SECRET' rubber stamped on his forehead and a banana in his mouth. The briefcase has gone.

DICK BARTON and JOCK enter.

DICK BARTON: (*Removing the banana.*) Good gracious, Colonel. What foreign infamy has happened here?

COLONEL GARDENER: Not in front of the lad, Barton. Top secret, don't you know.

DICK BARTON: Yes, better wait in the car, Jock.

JOCK: (*Taking out his Eagle comic.*) Rightie ho. (*He leaves.*)

COLONEL GARDENER: The bastard! The complete and utter bastard! He promised me he'd stop if I...

DICK BARTON: What are you talking about, old fellow? Who promised? Stop doing what?

COLONEL GARDENER: I don't think we need dwell on the details, Barton. All you need to know is that the briefcase containing the whereabouts of all our secret agents around the world has been stolen.

DICK BARTON: But you had it handcuffed to your wrist.

COLONEL GARDENER: They're very, very persuasive foreigners. Very clever. And to think I fell for it. Barton, I'm sure I don't have to say this, but not a word about it to the Minister. You know what he was like over the Grenadier Guard business.

DICK BARTON: With the brussel sprouts and the Jack Russell?

COLONEL GARDENER: No! Yes! It was a whippet! Look, the most important thing is you track down this devil.

DICK BARTON: I'll alert Scotland yard.

COLONEL GARDENER: Well... um, no. I wonder if you could clear up this matter yourself? Tip top classified information, and all that. We don't want to cause panic in the ranks. Young Jock can go to Argentina and rescue Rodger and Wilco, while you and Snowy stay here and track down my ruthless assailant.

BBC ANNOUNCER: And so it was, that as dawn broke over that capital of fair play and democracy, London Town, plucky Jock Anderson found himself, without sleep, about to board a plane for Argentina.

Scene 6

The airport.

JOCK is standing with his luggage, asleep on his feet, snoring with his mouth open.

TANNOY: (*Bing bong.*) Would passenger, Jock Anderson, please make your way urgently to gate three, where flight 408 to Buenos Aires International is about to board.

(*JOCK stays asleep.*)

(*Bing bong.*) Would passenger, Jock Anderson, please make way urgently to gate three, where flight 408 to Buenos Aires International is about to board.

(*JOCK stays asleep.*)

(*Bing bong.*) Would the little Scottish man by the WH Smith's, please pay attention!

(*JOCK wakes up.*)

Did you pack your bag yourself, sir?

JOCK: (*Clutches his bag.*) Mrs Horrocks put in some clean socks.

TANNOY: Any electrical equipment at all, sir?

JOCK: Aye, she's got a Hoover and a Goblin teasmaid.

TANNOY: Anything battery operated?

JOCK: I've no idea.

TANNOY: (*Bing bong.*) Please proceed immediately to gate three.

JOCK: Rightie Ho.

(*But as JOCK is about to exit...*)

Daphne?

DAPHNE: Oh! Jock! I...

JOCK: What on earth are you doing here?

DAPHNE: I...

JOCK: Och, you're not still following me are you? I'll be alright.

DAPHNE: Jock, I've been so worried. I can't help myself. When I didn't hear from you I... I was frightened.

JOCK: Didn't your butler give you my message?

DAPHNE: Oh, he's a rum old stick. I expect it slipped his mind.

JOCK: I see you've got your luggage with you.

DAPHNE: Um, yes.

JOCK: I'm sorry, I can't allow you to come with me.

DAPHNE: Really?

JOCK: I'm afraid not, lassie. This could be a very dangerous mission. Don't you realise some of these planes are going abroad. Think of the spicy food and different money.

DAPHNE: Heavens.

JOCK: No, I'm afraid I need you at home. So that whenever I'm in danger, I can picture you all safe and snug and warm, and it'll give me the strength to pull through.

DAPHNE: Oh darling, I'm so glad I can be of use.

JOCK: That's it. We've got to be brave.

DAPHNE: Oh Jock, I can't bear it. I can't bear not knowing where or when or…

JOCK: Hush, lassie. Just remember –

(JOCK and DAPHNE, with interjections from the TANNOY ANNOUNCER, sing a soppy wartime love song. At the end DAPHNE runs off tearfully. JOCK stifles a manly sob and exits to departure gate. JUAN enters with a suitcase.)

JUAN: Oi! Is everybody asleep in the bleedin' airport! I want to be on the next flight to Rio. Two tickets.

BBC ANNOUNCER: We do not know, we cannot guess, listeners, what mischief this criminal mastermind will plan, as he and his mystery companion gorge themselves on complimentary peanuts aboard the flight to Rio. But I can tell you that Reginald Hargrove, a listener from Tunbridge Wells, has rung in to point out that our Western concept of a preordained fate also finds parallels in older Eastern philosophies. And the lost property office on the Bakerloo line has called to say my brolly has turned up. Aboard Argentinian Airways flight 207, Jock Anderson settles back with the new *Eagle* comic, and ponders what adventures lie ahead for him in Argentina. Meanwhile, back at HQ, as Mrs Horrocks and Colonel Gardener anxiously await news of Dick Barton's manhunt, at least one mystery has been solved.

Scene 7

DICK BARTON's HQ.

COLONEL GARDENER, carrying a bottle of gin, joins MRS HORROCKS.

COLONEL GARDENER: I've found it. The cunning swine had hidden the bottle under the commode. Care for a stiff one, Mrs H?

MRS HORROCKS: Ooh no, Colonel. I can't relax knowing that somewhere in London there's a bomb set to explode if someone happens to think of the right tune.

COLONEL GARDENER: Just a small one. It'll help you relax.

MRS HORROCKS: I don't know whether I should. It doesn't agree with me. I only have to so much as sniff a cork and I'm like a giggling school girl of fifteen.

COLONEL GARDENER: How delightful. (*Hands her a drink.*) You deserve to let your hair down a little.

MRS HORROCKS: (*Coy.*) Oh well, don't say I didn't warn you. Now you will excuse any skittishness won't you, you naughty man.
(*MRS HORROCKS takes a slug of gin and is transformed into an aggressive, loud, ugly, vulgar drunk.*)
The bastard. All men are bastards! He comes round here again with his fancy talk and I'll rip his head off, the continental Dago slime bucket. Love, don't talk to me about love, it makes me puke!
(*The COLONEL also takes a drink. It makes him loud and morose.*)

COLONEL GARDENER: Ain't that the truth, sister!

MRS HORROCKS: I would have given him everything! Everything!

COLONEL GARDENER: It's never enough, is it?

MRS HORROCKS: You're not wrong there, it's never a-bleedin'-nough. He treated me like a princess.

COLONEL GARDENER: They always do.

MRS HORROCKS: Like a princess! And then, when he got what he wanted, you didn't see him for dust.

COLONEL GARDENER: They're only after one thing.

MRS HORROCKS: Same thing happened to my sister.

COLONEL GARDENER: Really?

MRS HORROCKS: Oh, yes. Seduced by an Argy banana trader on the docks at Wapping. Promised her the earth but the next day he set sail for Argentina. She got the next boat after him and we never heard from her again. She was happy, engaged to a lovely lad from the co-op she was, had a good job too, mopping out the conveniences at Catford Dog Track. But it only took a few honeyed lies from that swarthy, handsome son of a bitch, and she chucked it all in.

COLONEL GARDENER: That's terrible.

MRS HORROCKS: You'd have thought I'd have learnt wouldn't you? But, no! Matey comes in here with his piercing eyes, broad shoulders and slim snake-like hips, and I was completely at his mercy. It was that tune that did it.

COLONEL GARDENER: Ah yes, there's always a tune. That's how they hook you. A stray piece of coal black hair unfurls itself in the nape of the neck, perhaps you catch the exotic whiff of danger, and then the music starts.

(*He moves to the piano and starts to play the vamp intro to The Tune. Just as he is about to go into the main section, which will detonate the bomb, he stops.*)

MRS HORROCKS: Please Colonel, don't stop.

COLONEL GARDENER: I have to. That tune, it brings back so many painful memories.

MRS HORROCKS: (*Gently.*) Here I'll help you, maybe it'll help chase away a few ghosts.

· (*They play as a duet, first of all gently and romantically and then they swing it.*
DICK BARTON and SNOWY burst in.)

SNOWY: Oooh, I love a sing song. (*He sings tunelessly.*)

DICK BARTON: Stop! Stop at once!

COLONEL GARDENER: Barton! Have you found my assailant?

DICK BARTON: Never mind about that now! Listen!

SNOWY: What?

MRS HORROCKS: There's a ticking noise coming from the vase.

DICK BARTON: Run!

(*Blackout.*

A huge explosion.

Lights up on the four amongst the wreckage.)

MRS HORROCKS: Thank heavens you got us out in time, Mr Barton.

SNOWY: I'll get started clearing up, shall I? (*He goes.*)

DICK BARTON: That tune you were playing. It must have triggered the bomb.

COLONEL GARDENER: Great heavens. It was the tune that the man who robbed me was whistling.

MRS HORROCKS: It was the tune the heartless swine who broke my heart was whistling.

DICK BARTON: I don't want anyone to get too excited, but I think a pattern is emerging. If only we knew if it was the same tune that Rodger and Wilco gave to Snowy at Lords.

COLONEL GARDENER: Jock will find out.

DICK BARTON: Yes, I just pray he reaches them before the agents of EFIL. If we can link everything together, I've got a pretty good idea who's behind all this.

(*The sound of sawing from off.*)

(*Calls.*) Stop those repairs now, Snowy. You and I have got a date with danger. Mrs Horrocks will sort things out here. Colonel, listen very carefully. I want you to book Snowy and I on to the next flight to Rio de Janeiro. Get in touch with Jock and tell him to confirm the code tune Rodger and Wilco gave to Snowy. Make sure they're on their way to safety, and then have him meet us at the International Conference of Cinema Organists in Brazil.

COLONEL GARDENER: The International Conference of – ?

DICK BARTON: No time to explain, old fellow.

COLONEL GARDENER: By God, you're good, Barton.

DICK BARTON: Only doing my job, Colonel. Mrs H? (*He looks round at the mess.*) Good luck with the clear up.

(*The men go. MRS HORROCKS rolls up her sleeves and swigs the last drop of gin in the bottle.*)

MRS HORROCKS: Right! Where's the Brasso?

(*She finds it in her apron pocket and has a swig.*)

BBC ANNOUNCER: Oh dear! So much is riding on the broad shoulders of Jock Anderson. But things are not going so well, as he searches the back streets of Buenos Aires for Secret Agents Rodger and Wilco.

Scene 8

The street and then CONCHITA HORROCKS' café.

JOCK: Och, I can't make head nor tail of this wee map. Just my luck that they'd run out of street guides to Buenos Aires. I shouldn't have believed the man when he said that the one for Barcelona would do just as well. I'm tired and homesick and missing my wee gal. I wonder if you can get a cup of tea around here. Och, look at that wee café. 'English spoken here'. 'A taste of home' 'Overcooked soggy veg, a speciality.' What a life saver. I must admit it looks pretty run down. They can't have had a customer in years. (*Looks at the name over the door.*) 'Conchita Horrocks.' Well, that's got a reassuring ring about it.

(*He enters the filthy cobweb strewn café of CONCHITA HORROCKS. Leaning against the counter are two of her surly daughters, MAUREEN and MARGARITA.*)

MAUREEN: A man!

MARGARITA: (*Calls off.*) Mamma, mamma, a man!

JOCK: I wonder if I could get a nice cup of tea, and do you do porridge by any chance?

MAUREEN: And he's English.

JOCK: Well, I'm from Scotland actually.

(*The girls break off into an aggressive sounding Argentinian babble discussing this. Then they turn and smile at him.*)

MAUREEN: Is the same thing.

MARGARITA: Mamma, mamma! At last, one has come into the shop.

MAUREEN: We got one!

(*CONCHITA HORROCKS bursts in. She has a rifle at her side, hair piled on top of her head, is covered in flounces, and has a cigar in her mouth. She is flanked by her other two daughters, CASSANDRA and YVETTE, who look lustfully at JOCK.*)

CONCHITA HORROCKS: At last, this time the plan has worked.

CASSANDRA/YVETTE: Mamma! Is he what we're looking for?

CONCHITA HORROCKS: Oh yes! It's the real thing this time. Look at those legs. Bolt the door.

JOCK: Good day, Madam. It says outside you do English cooking.

CONCHITA HORROCKS: It's true. It is my specialty. I come from England long ago. I was tricked by a banana tradesman. He did me wrong.

(*All the DAUGHTERS spit on the floor.*)

He left me with my four beautiful daughters and this broken down shop, and took off with a double-jointed Cuban trapeze artist.

DAUGHTERS: Bitch! (*They spit.*)

CONCHITA HORROCKS: I swore that my daughters would never suffer as I have, in the arms of some no good Argentinian man. So, I adopted my sister's married name to ward off any more latino scum, and I open this place to lure good Englishmen to be their husbands. They doubted me, but now, look girls – ten years later, a customer. (*Pointing the rifle at JOCK.*) Which one you going to marry?

JOCK: To marry? But…

CONCHITA HORROCKS: Silence! You want to take a look?

EINE KLEINE TANGO

(*Sings.*) Hey, you want to dance with pretty girls?
Mama's here to show her string of pearls.

MAUREEN: I'm Maureen and I'm the Tango queen
Hold me close I'll show you what I mean.

Lock hips, and learn my Tango tips.
When you desire me, it really fires me
And soon you'll treasure, without measure
Every pleasured, leisured night.
So why fight me? Just ignite me
I've decided with one look at you you're Mr Right.
Feel me quiver, see me shiver
I just look at you and want to bite your bum –
Tiddley-un-pum-pum
Just pay my mum
A modest, fair, pre-nuptial sum.
And then you'll quickly learn
How hot a love can burn.

DAUGHTERS: (*Except MAUREEN.*) Get off, you've had your turn.

(*A fight breaks out. Then they remember themselves, smile at jock, and MARGARITA steps forward.*)

MARGARITA: My name is Margarita
I too have dancing feet – a
Nimble footed Fellah
Could win my tarantella
Glide across the room
Say you'll be a groom.
And then let's bang till it's obscene
Upon my little tambourine

JOCK: (*Spoken.*) I don't think you understand... Please let me explain...

CONCHITA HORROCKS: How's the show? I trust that you approve?
Don't be shy girls, show him how you move.

YVETTE: P'raps you want to dance with your Yvette
I will Rumba any chance I get.
Who's glum when there's a Bongo drum?
I'm in my element, the rhythm's heaven sent
It's idiotic, but erotic and exotic melodies
Make me giggle, make me wriggle
Make me start to tremble and I weaken at the knees.
I can do the same for you

Just take a gander at the
Marriage contract please.
You stole my heart
Read up until the small print starts
Just sign it now
Come here I'll show you how

DAUGHTERS: (*Except YVETTE.*) Give up you pushy cow!
(*Another fight.*)

CASSANDRA: They call me Big Cassandra
I like to dance the Samba
My sisters all are crackers
But don't have my maracas

CONCHITA HORROCKS: Dance my darlings, dance!
Take another glance.

ALL THE WOMEN: Pick a Latin lovely Honey
Now's the perfect chance.
Ole!

CONCHITA HORROCKS: (*Pointing the gun.*) Now! You
choose!

JOCK: I think you're all very bonny lasses.

CONCHITA HORROCKS: (*Pleased.*) You want all! Maybe
you take Mamma Horrocks, too!

JOCK: No, no you don't understand. You see, much as I'd
love to marry any one of you beautiful ladies, I can't.

CONCHITA HORROCKS: (*Points gun.*) You have dirty
disease. Maureen! Get the ointment!
(*MAUREEN exits.*)

JOCK: Och, no, it's nothing like that. You see I already
have a sweetheart. And if I were to marry one of you I
could never make you happy, because even if I tried
really hard to love you it could never work. That wee
girl back home she's captured my heart and deep down
inside I could never give my love to any one else in the
whole wide world. So I hope you won't be offended when
I say thank you very much but no. I'll just take a hot cup
of milky tea and a bowl of porridge. Salt not sugar.
(*The girls are very moved by this sincere little speech.*)

CONCHITA HORROCKS: Oh, that's so beautiful. Why
can't we find men like this instead of *pigs!*

(*They spit.*)

I'll go and warm the pot. (*She exits.*)

YVETTE: Please forgive Mamma, she only wants the best for us.

JOCK: I can see that. She reminds me of our housekeeper back home in England.

CASSANDRA: Oh, England. How we long to see it. The Leaning Tower Of London, the changing of the beef eaters –

MARGARITA: Arthur Askey.

YVETTE: He funny man, no?

JOCK: Och yes, he has us in stitches.

CASSANDRA: So what brings you to Buenos Aires, Mr – ?

JOCK: Jock, Jock Anderson. Well, I'm here on business. I have to track down two friends of mine. They could be in great danger.

MARGARITA: You are so brave.

YVETTE: Tell us Mr Jock, do you have brothers at home you could send us?

JOCK: Well, I can certainly ask Granny McNair if she can spare any more of us. It can get quite busy on the farm. Especially when there's Aberdeen Angus breeding.

CASSANDRA: We like the sound of him! You put Mr Angus on plane to us, yes?

MARGARITA: So good to meet a real Englishman. The only other two who come by. They were no use to us.

YVETTE: They big disappointment.

CASSANDRA: All Judy Garland this and Judy Garland that!

MARGARITA: (*On the bright side.*) But still they teach Mamma how to make quiche.

YVETTE: And I know never to accessorise that handbag with that scarf again.

JOCK: Just a minute. These two Englishmen. What did they look like?

CASSANDRA: They'll be back soon and you can see. They rented the room above the kitchen.

JOCK: Och, heaven be praised. Please, please let it be.

(*We see RODGER and WILCO approaching.*)

RODGER: Well, another job well done, Wiggy.

WILCO: I should say so, Rodg.

RODGER: They'll think twice about flogging their –

BOTH: – dodgy corned beef –

RODGER: – on the English black market again.

WILCO: And weren't those Comanchero lads helpful?

RODGER: They certainly were. I know you'll be taking home very fond memories of –

BOTH: – big Pedro.

JOCK: Rodger! Wilco!

BOTH: It's Jock!

WILCO: What on earth –

BOTH: – are you doing here?

JOCK: I've come to warn you. The forces of EFIL have stolen the file detailing your whereabouts. Colonel Gardener reckons they're sending a hit man to kill you.

RODGER: Didn't I say this would happen?

WILCO: You certainly did, darling.

RODGER: Was our swarthy –

BOTH: – tango friend with the whistle –

RODGER: – behind all this?

JOCK: I don't know. Snowy couldn't sing us the tune you gave him. I'm worried I won't be able to do much better.

WILCO: Of course you will. Yvette, you keep a look out for any potential hit men.

(*YVETTE leaves.*)

Margarita and Cassandra –

RODGER: – let's teach Jock –

BOTH: – the special tune:

NOTES TO SING

When you've learnt the notes to sing,
You'll remember anything:
G – G – G
G – F#* – E – F# – G – A
B – B – B

*F# pronounced as F in lyrics, not F#.

B – A – G – A – B – C
D – G
E – D – C – B – A – G !

JOCK: Could you just repeat that?

RODGER: Absolotomento!

(*They repeat it and they dance.*)

RODGER/WILCO: Now you try.

(*JOCK has a go and nearly gets it but stumbles over the last bit.*)

JOCK: What was the last bit again?

WILCO: Come on, girls. Let's show him how it's done.

(*They do.*)

JOCK: Oh, you mean – ?

(*He does as they did.*)

RODGER: All together now.

(*They all sing and dance.*

Before the last verse, the sound of a phone ringing. Everyone looks around for where the noise is coming from. WILCO leaves.

RODGER, with JOCK and the GIRLS, listen into an object that turns out to be a telephone.)

(*Spoken.*) It's HQ in London. Jock, you're to go to the Hotel International Rio De Janiero. Wiggy and I have got a new secret mission in Jamaica involving Princess Margaret and an H bomb test. Now, one more time, Jock, how does the tune go?

(*Big finish to the number.*)

BBC ANNOUNCER: And so with the jaunty tune imbedded in the long-term memory of the tartan sleuth, the plucky lad begins the next step of his journey into mystery and adventure. An adventure which now builds to a nail-biting climax in the beneath the Riba! Riba! Ooondalay! Picture House Rio De Janeiro.

Scene 9

In the cellars beneath a cinema in Rio.

Darkness.

DICK BARTON: Ah darkness, the inky cloak of blackness that shields the work of EFIL from the right thinking world, even as it cradles the sleeping innocent in its cool caress. Will there ever come a time when man can give in to its call to sleep, sleep deep in its black velvet arms, safe in the knowledge that nothing nasty lies waiting under the bed or behind the wardrobe door?

SNOWY: I'll pop the light on then, shall I?

DICK BARTON: Not yet, old friend. We've plans to make before we give ourselves away.

SNOWY: I don't think I like it here in Rio, Guv.

DICK BARTON: Why's that, Snowy?

SNOWY: I'm getting prickly heat. Either that or the month's come round again to change me long johns.

DICK BARTON: Not to worry old chap, we'll soon be back in Blighty again. I've a sense the case of The Tango of Terror is about to come to a conclusion.

SNOWY: What are we doing underneath this creepy old cinema?

DICK BARTON: Not just any cinema, old chap. Do you recall why the Riba! Riba! Ooondalay! Picture House is the toast of Rio?

SNOWY: Do they let pensioners in cheap on a Wednesday?

DICK BARTON: Think man, think! We are in the home of the biggest upright organ in the free world. It is from here, below the screen that the majestic beast rises up to bring musical relief to the jaded ears of Brazilian Cinema Goers. (*He shines his torch at the organ.*)

SNOWY: I've seen bigger.

DICK BARTON: Don't be deceived by the trick of the half light, Snowy. That fellow's a big 'un alright. we're just standing a long way away from it. By god it's a beauty. They come from all over the world to marvel at this beast. So where better then here, to stage this year's international conference of cinema organists? Gathering in the auditorium above, from all four corners of the earth, are men who ride their mighty wurlitzers in public.

SNOWY: I've never trusted them organists, brightly coloured blazers, cheesy grins.

DICK BARTON: Precisely. And since last week we have all the more reason to be suspicious.

SNOWY: Why's that, DB?

DICK BARTON: Oh Snowy, you young pup, I despair of you. How often do I have to tell you? If you want to be a top special agent you need to read *The Times* everyday from cover to cover. If you'd read last Wednesday, a small item on page twenty-five would have caught your eye and alerted you to potential danger. At their last meeting the members of ISCO – the International Society of Cinema Organists – unanimously elected Londoner, Juan El Bigglesworth, as their new leader. Surely that infamous name rings a bell?

SNOWY: Yes, it does! I went to school with him. His dad lost his marbles and Juan went to the bad. I saw him the other day at the cricket.

DICK BARTON: Did you indeed. I don't doubt it. And did you happen to tell him the address of our HQ?

SNOWY: Now you come to mention it, I think I did. Has he popped round yet?

DICK BARTON: Oh yes, he popped round all right and he left a fearful lot of explosives as a calling card! It is tonight at this very conference that he will make his inaugural speech. Tradition dictates that the new leader makes his first entrance, rising up through the floor at the keyboard of a mighty cinema organ, like this one. And so you see why it was so important that we came here.

SNOWY: Um, no.

DICK BARTON: Not to worry, old chap.

JUAN: (*Off.*) Pass round the cheesy nibbles upstairs, whilst I position myself at the organ. Give me a few moments to rehearse my speech and then bring me up through the floor.

DICK BARTON: Quick, hide.

(*SNOWY and BARTON hide.*

JUAN enters, looking very 'Phantom-of-the-Opera'. He sits at the organ and plays a quick blast of 'I Do Like to Be Beside the Seaside', then grins over his shoulder in that cheesy way cinema organists used to. He swivels around on the stool as if to address his conference.)

JUAN: Fellow organists, welcome, one and all. (*He changes his mind, takes out his speech and makes a correction.*) Fellow organists *and your good lady wives*, welcome one and all. You all know me I hope. It's good to see so many familiar faces who over the years visited my father in Peckham for advice and guidance on cinema organ repertoire. I don't have to remind you of the tragedy that befell my sainted father; he died a broken man in a year that should have seen his greatest triumph and his becoming a millionaire. Now ruin faces us all. From around the world, I have heard horror stories of cinema organs being ripped out and your services being replaced by gramophone records. But fear not, I have devised a plan that will save us all. It combines my mother's greed for jewellery with my father's musical genius. We will form ourselves into vicious gangs who hide behind cinema screens around the world…

(*From their hiding place.*)

SNOWY: DB!

DICK BARTON: It's just as I feared. I'll take care of things here. You go and radio for some reinforcements.

(*SNOWY sneaks out.*)

JUAN: …When one of our remaining organist colleagues plays my father's tune, it will signal that the doors have been bolted and security distracted. We will leap out, steal cash and jewellery from the audience, and take them hostage until governments all around the world grant us our hearts' desire. With the British Secret Service paralysed by my efforts for EFIL over these last few months there's no one to stop us.

DICK BARTON: (*Coming out of hiding with a gun.*) Not so fast, El Bigglesworth. I'm afraid British Intelligence is on to you. You'll be making a very different speech tonight with me at your side. When you greet your colleagues now, it will be with your hands raised above your head, as you lead your ruthless cohorts in a legally binding renouncement of EFIL, or I'm afraid it's prison for you all.

JUAN: Dick Barton, you're a bigger fool than I thought. I am a mere cog in EFIL's wheel. Do not underestimate the cruel genius that really controls tonight's machinations. I think you'll find her a formidable opponent.

DICK BARTON: Ah ha! I should have known you weren't brilliant enough to come up with this criminal masterplan all on your own. No, El Bigglesworth, you're strictly small time aren't you? So there's a deadly female pulling the strings. Marta Heartburn! It's her twisted mind that is behind all this, isn't it?

JUAN: What a fool you are Barton, and what a fitting tribute tonight will be to Daddy's memory. Ruthless killers are posted at every entrance to this building. You won't get out of here alive. And I know the very tune with which to herald your death.
(*JUAN plays The Tune – sounding huge and gothic on the mighty cinema organ.*)

JOCK: (*Bursting in.*) DB! DB! That's the tune. That's the tune that has haunted our whole investigation.

DICK BARTON: I know it is, old chap. If I'm honest, I suspected it was this blood-curdling piece for a while now. Don't think EFIL has triumphed El Bigglesworth.

JOCK: I bring terrible news, DB. We're done for this time. EFIL have outsmarted us. British secret agents have been captured around the world and are being held to ransom. Snowy, and all your back-up here, has been intercepted by international terrorists and just this minute, His Majesty received a demand that we hand over the crown jewels and Arthur Askey's head by midnight, or Britain will be invaded by foreign anarchists.

DICK BARTON: Tricky.

JOCK: Isn't it.

DICK BARTON: What kind of mistress of infamy can be behind this ruthless catalogue of horror?

    (*DAPHNE steps out of the shadows with a gun.*)

DAPHNE: Hello Mr. Barton. Hello Jock.

JOCK: (*Casually.*) Oh hello darling, this could get a bit nasty, why don't you wait upstairs by the popcorn?

DAPHNE: I don't think you quite understand, Jock. I never was your darling. I was simply trying to trick you to your death. With you out of the way, EFIL could be a step closer to its ultimate goal – the murder of one who had so often thwarted their plans: Dick Barton.

JOCK: But why would you get yourself mixed up in all this?

DAPHNE: For the love of my Juan, my Latin love thug. I fell for him that night at the Hammersmith Palais, the one they call El Bigglesworth. When he told me of his tragic family history, I devised this whole scheme for our glorious future together.

JOCK: How will I keep my heart from breaking?

DICK BARTON: You won't get away with this.

DAPHNE: And just how will you stop us, Mr Barton?

JUAN: Yes, how are you going to get out of this one?

DICK BARTON: There's only one-way to find out –

JOCK: What's that?

BBC ANNOUNCER: Tune in to the next exciting instalment of:

EVERYONE: Dick Barton, Special Agent.

The End.